Mike Hall was born in Hastings, East Sussex and enlisted as a 'Boy Drummer' straight from school aged fifteen into the Coldstream Guards in the winter of 1959. Having enjoyed Christmas of that year at home, he reported to the Junior Guardsmans' Company, Pirbright camp on the 8th January 1960 to begin his basic military training. Following this his music training began in earnest covering both practical musicianship and music theory; training which would stand him in good stead in later years for writing and arranging music for corps of drums. Following a twelve-month tour on active service with the 2nd Battalion in South Arabia he was posted to the prestigious Guards Depot Corps of Drums as Second-in-Command, thereafter being selected for posting to the Junior Guardsmens' Company on promotion to full Sergeant as Senior Instructor. It was during this time that his creative pen began to flourish to good effect with 'Drummers of the Queen'. The appointment as Drum Major to the First Battalion followed, a post he was to hold until electing to 'go to duty' – this led to various postings to the Royal Military Academy Sandhurst (RMAS), firstly as Company Sergeant Major Instructor and later as College Regimental Sergeant Major of New College, these postings being interspersed with routine public duties and operational tours of Northern Ireland. On commissioning into the regiment he served as Mechanical Transport Officer and Technical Quarter Master (TQM) and then as the last Quartermaster of the Second Battalion upon its demise. Once again he was posted to the RMAS as TQM. It was during this latter posting that he was selected as the Army's nomination to establish from scratch, the central Army training organisation then titled Drums/GPMG(SF) Company based at Helles Barracks, Catterick; a post which required him (with characteristic fortitude) to attend and pass the GPMG (SF) Commanders' course at Brecon, Powys at the age of fifty.

He retired from the Army in the rank of Major in October 2000 having served for forty years, the first nineteen years as a 'drummer'. Mike never lost touch with the Drums and with the support of Colonel Peter Walton and Major Richard Powell was responsible for overseeing and devising such occasions as massed drums for the Lord Mayor's Show, the Wembley Tattoos and the outstanding display of a massed corps of drums and bugles of the Light Division at the final Royal Tournament.

During his work with the Drums he has, with the assistance of Major Richard Powell, masterminded several recordings, all of which carry evidence of his ability to write and arrange music for the genre. One CD reviewed was awarded 'CD of the month' by the late Col Rodney Bashford in *Gramophone* magazine.

A co-author of the *Drummers' Handbook*, Mike also wrote the *Drums' Instructors Manual*, the *Arranging Pamphlet* and also created training objectives and test specifications for Regular Army at Class 1, 2 and 3 and likewise for the Army Cadet Force (ACF) and Combined Cadet Force (CCF) for drum, fife and bugle as part of the star qualification system levels one to four, all of which are official Army publications. He continues to maintain close contact with the Drums through the Corps of Drums Society in the role of Training Development Officer and Technical Advisor dealing with related drum and flute matters.

"I am not a musician, so if I speak as a barbarian I must ask you to forgive me. From the lowest point of view a few drums and fifes in a battalion means at least five extra miles in a route march, quite apart from the fact that they can swing a battalion back to quarters happy and composed in its mind, no matter how wet or tired its body may be. Even when there is no route marching, the mere come and go, the roll and flourishing of drums and fifes around the barracks is as warming and cheering as the sight of a fire in a room".

Rudyard Kipling

The Drummers' Code
"To strive, in all things, to create the situation where excellence is the norm and only the absence of censure is construed as praise."

After Col David Murray

WITH TRUMPET, DRUM AND FIFE

A SHORT TREATISE COVERING THE RISE AND FALL OF MILITARY MUSICAL INSTRUMENTS ON THE BATTLEFIELD

Helion Studies in Military History no 22

Major Mike Hall

Helion & Company Ltd

Helion & Company Limited
26 Willow Road
Solihull
West Midlands
B91 1UE
England
Tel. 0121 705 3393
Fax 0121 711 4075
Email: info@helion.co.uk
Website: www.helion.co.uk

Published by Helion & Company 2013

Designed and typeset by Farr out Publications, Wokingham, Berkshire
Cover designed by the author
Printed by Lightning Source Ltd, Milton Keynes, Buckinghamshire

© Major Mike Hall 2013

ISBN 978-1-909384-17-0

British Library Cataloguing-in-Publication Data.
A catalogue record for this book is available from the British Library.

All rights reserved. No part of this publication may be reproduced, stored in a retrieval system, or transmitted, in any form, or by any means, electronic, mechanical, photocopying, recording or otherwise, without the express written consent of Helion & Company Limited.

For details of other military history titles published by Helion & Company Limited contact the above address, or visit our website: http://www.helion.co.uk.

We always welcome receiving book proposals from prospective authors.

Contents

List of illustrations		vii
Acknowledgements		9
Introduction		10

Part I   The Ancient World
- 1. Early Accounts of Trumpets and Drums in Military Use   12
- 2. Other Percussion Instruments   16
- 3. Other Influences on Military Music   18
- 4. Grecian Influence   20
- 5. Roman Influence in Britain – Roman Brass Instruments   22
- 6. Post Romano-Britain, the Saxons and the Vikings   27
- 7. 1066 and Onwards – the Norman Conquest   28

Part II   From the Waytes to Cromwell
- 8. Elevated Status – Privileges and Pecking Order   32
- 9. Influence of the Crusades on English Martial Instruments   35
- 10. A New Order – Foundations of a Standing Army   37
- 11. Drum and Fife Commands – Posture and Motions   41
- 12. The Old English March – Importance of the Drum   43
- 13. Dating the Existence of the Post of Drum Major   48
- 14. Cromwell – the Commonwealth and its Influence   49

Part III   The Restoration and Beyond
- 15. The Serjeant Trumpeter and Drum Major General   55
- 16. Last of the 'Sovereign Generals'   56
- 17. Post-Napoleon   58
- 18. TA to the Rescue – The Corps of Drums Society   63
- 19. The Phoenix Arises – the Rebirth of the Drum Major General   64

Part IV   Origins and Development of Instruments
- 20. Origins, Development, Music and the Use of Trumpet and Bugle   67
- 21. Bugles and Trumpets at War   73
- 22. Development of the Side Drum   82
- 23. Development of the Fife   86

Part V	Dress and Duties	
	24. Dress	91
	25. Drummers and Military Discipline	97
	26. Blackamoors as Drummers	100
	27. The Drum Major – a Historical Precedent	102
	28. The English Duty – Drum and Flute Duty	105
Coda		111
Sources Cited		112

List of illustrations

The Stele (monument) to Naram Sin showing the king towering over his enemies during a successful mountain campaign. The question remains is that a wounded soldier trying to remove an arrow from his throat or is it a trumpeter defiantly sounding to the last breath?   13

Sacred icons – clearly of Jewish origin being transported away from the sacked and destroyed Temple of Jerusalem following the Hebrew/Roman wars of AD70. Note – amongst these sacred items are two metal trumpets. (By kind permission of OUP.)   14

Young Greek aulos player – Many of these would be assembled into a 'corps' which would be positioned immediately behind the leading battle formations – literally to play the Hoplites to war.   21

An excellent example of a carved relief located on Trajan's Column showing Roman soldiers carrying and playing cornu – noticeably the largest of the Roman brass instruments.   23

Three carnyxes embossed on the Gundestrup Cauldron (extreme right) discovered in a peat bog in Denmark and said to be dated between 200 BC and 300 AD and fashioned in pure silver.   24

A copy of the percussion parts which served as an introduction to the funeral marches of Beethoven, Chopin and Handel – beaten by 75 massed drums and bass drums for the Funeral of Edward VII on 24th May 1910.   33

From a work by Francis Sandford – The History of the Coronation of James II – This woodcut of the Coronation procession of James II in 1685 shows the four drummers of the Royal household lead by a fife player whose fife is decked with a bannerol.   34

A drummer of the 17th century – Note the dimensions of the drum and weighty sticks, the slashed over-sleeve at the shoulders of his tunic (which possibly developed into wings worn by drummers today) the silk sash – perhaps the fore-runner of the cross belt worn by Drum Majors, also the officers feather on his cap. Clearly dressed up to a standard and not down to a price!   42

17th century fifer – Note slashed over-sleeve, silk sash and feather in the cap. Note too the length of the fife and the carriage of a sword. He appears to be playing his fife 'back to front' but this may be a mistake by the woodcutter. See the illustration of mounted fifers for a similar oddity.   42

Posture and motions, fife tunes – to which musket drills and firing postures were performed to the signalling beat of the drum and fife.   43

A copy of the Old English March as pricked down by Edward Norgate – *Windsor Herald*.   44

A Bone fragment recovered from an ancient Neanderthal campsite, which is claimed to be the remains of a flute.   87

VIII WITH TRUMPET, DRUM AND FIFE

Chinese flutes from 9,000 years BC – note the standard design of six finger holes and one embouchure – the latter being the same size as the finger holes – all made from hollowed out bird bones. (Courtesy of Brookhaven National Laboratory)   87

From a woodcut showing a rare example of mounted fifers as depicted in the 'Triumph of Maximilian I (1526)' – The Triumph refers to a book of 137 engravings. Note each fifer carries a fife case at his belt to accommodate at least three differently pitched fifes. Paradoxically, one of the three fifers appears to be playing left handed – not impossible, but most unusual.   88

This illustration highlights some of the developments in simple system flute design. Note the metal head joint complete with tuning slide and the cylindrical bore. The creation of the 'chimney' in this case, is achieved by a lip plate.   88

A major development in fife making was the shaping and depth of the embouchure. This change from concentric to ovoid, created greater sonority and power in the lower register.   88

This illustration shows a modern six-key simple system flute, as used by Swiss drum and flute bands to this day. It is a highly versatile instrument pitched in Concert 'C'. With the improved embouchure and the conical bore, it allows for greater power in the lower register with clarity and precision of tone in the upper register.   88

It may be seen from the illustration of the fife that the external body of the fife widens out to about 22mm in the area of the embouchure. This allows for sufficient wall thickness to create the necessary 'chimney', which forms the correct depth of the embouchure from the exterior to the surface of the inner bore.   88

Acknowledgements

Special mention must be made of Sheila Hope whose contribution in the typing, layout, design and seemingly constant reams of author generated typos, she uncomplainingly bore with a sense of humour and professionalism oft-times tried;

Colonel Peter Walton and Major Richard Powell for their long term help and advice; Dr Maurice Byrne for his permission to use work on the English March; Colonel David Murray for the Drummers' Code; John Ambler (formerly Royal Marines) for information concerning the Drum Major General; the Corps of Drums Society; and, ultimately, Sarah and the family for putting up with my domination of the computer

Front cover photography – Harvey Hall, layout and design – Ross McSherry.

Introduction

A large part of the text for this book started out its life as a set of lecture notes used on such occasions as talks to members of the International Military Music Society (IMMS), The Corps of Drums Society, the Northern Ireland marching bands movement in Belfast hosted by the Mourne Young Defenders and a series of lectures to each of the newly formed student bandmasters' courses regarding the history of and the principles of writing and arranging music for corps of drums. The latter series of these lectures was conducted at Kneller Hall by invitation of Major Gordon Turner, who was then on the professorial staff at the school.

This document seeks in no way to be a detailed history of the Ancient world, however, certain parts of it have been selected, used and quoted more by way of a vehicle to demonstrate the development and use of drums, fifes, war horns and, later, trumpets in certain of the great civilisations at war, initially Egypt, Persia, Greece and Rome. Other examples will occur from time to time with descriptions of some of their land battles, setting the scene whereby the reader has the opportunity to exercise their imagination and join the roller-coaster of historic conflict and battlefield signalling, often in pursuit of creating vast empires over which to rule.

The writer is not a historian and history being what it is will confound anyone who attempts to unravel the 'Gordian Knot'- in consequence, history becomes enshrined in folk lore and legend, built upon the shifting sands of rumour or hearsay. Wherever hypothesis is to be found in this book, the writer has allowed for this eventuality and has declared it in the text. Similarly, where one is on solid ground dealing with well documented and researched factual events and actions, these are offered as such and may be accepted as 'bona fide' and may well form the basis for a consensus of informed discussion at future 'drums events, mayhap over a flagon or two. Doubtless there will be those of a cavilistic nature who will carp at some detail or other – so be it!

The origins of percussion instruments and the creation of the drum, in whatever form it first manifested itself, are mysteries that remain some distance beyond being answerable. It is likely that it is as old as the ascent of man. Some early indication of the existence of a percussion instrument named the 'Drum of the Earth'- is hinted at in Professor James Blade's *Percussion Instruments and Their History*. This drum (sic) is said to have been constructed of two conical holes in the ground, fashioned in hard baked mud or clay, these when being beaten using the open palm of the hand – acted as a resonator. Think also in addition to this, an animal skin stretched out and pegged down to dry in the sun and the hunter, tapping it with a stick to test its state, finds to his pleasure that in drying, the skin has tightened and now produces an interesting sound. Consider a pot or gourd, having stretched over it a skin membrane to keep out the bugs or rodents; this when struck, also producing a satisfying sound or the fascination of the sound of dried beans or stones rattled in a pot or even the reverberation of hollow tree trunks amplifying sound when beaten with sticks. Predating even this is a percussion instrument more basic, which has survived history and remains prolific to this day, and used to demonstrate adulation, approbation, dissatisfaction or greeting. It is of course, the sound produced by the clapping of hands.

In these possible actions we might begin to see the development of early percussion instruments and from these humble beginnings comes a clear understanding by primitive man, of the fundamental principle that a satisfying sound could be produced from the percussive striking of one object against another; furthermore, it demonstrated a basic awareness that open vessels could produce even more satisfying and amplified sounds when struck. It would not have been too long perhaps, before a vessel say, would have been deliberately fitted with a tightened skin membrane in order to produce the desired sound for its own sake.

It is often postulated that the drum as we understand it today, did not come into military use in England until after the Crusades. In general terms this is probably so but, it is held by the writer that a new range of percussion instruments, in fairly sophisticated form and bearing evidence of snare fittings, was most likely to have been introduced by the Romans in 55-54 BC during their first and somewhat comparatively short invasion and occupation of Britain under Julius Caesar. It is believed that Roman percussion instruments were largely used in domestic and entertainment roles but militarily, used only on the march. The dominant Roman military signalling instrument on the battlefield, like so many great armies before them, was the trumpet, which along with the fife and drum will form a part of this study.

For years it has been accepted by almost everyone connected with military drumming that the drum, in one form or another, the trumpet and the fife have been used as signalling instruments on the battlefield. Furthermore, it is also assumed that those who beat upon the drum, sounded the trumpet or played the fife were of good personage, literate and capable men, specially chosen and licensed.

All this begs the questions – Is it true? Upon what basis was this alleged importance founded? When did it all begin? It is to these questions that this book will address itself and also attempt to give an insight into the development of accoutrements, dress and the art of drumming and a look at its current role and status in the Foot Guards and Regiments of the Infantry of the Line – Segue!

Part I

The Ancient World

1. Early Accounts of Trumpets and Drums in Military Use

Some possible evidence of early use of the trumpet on the battlefield is to be seen on the monument or 'stele', erected to mark the glorious victories of a fighting emperor from 2000 BC. The Stele of Naram-Sin (grandson of Sargon the first – conqueror of Sumeria and creator of the first true Empire of Mesopotamia) shows him trampling his enemies to death following the execution of a successful mountain campaign. More importantly, it depicts what to some appears to be a trumpeter at the centre of battle defiantly sounding his trumpet to the last (though some sources claim that the figure depicted represents a defeated soldier attempting to pull an arrow from his neck) – regardless of the military role to which he might be consigned whether soldier or trumpeter he too, is about to be trampled; of more significance, (if he is indeed a trumpeter) is the style of trumpet shown. It is clearly of the type created by manufacture and not fashioned from the keratin sleeve of an animal horn. It bears saying that the support for the arrow theory shows it to be an uncommonly long missile for an arrow. Closer inspection gives the impression that there is a slight flare towards the bell (sic.) so possibly here might be seen evidence of fairly advanced metal working; also its tube length in particular, indicating the possible harmonic range achievable.

Further back in history and prior to Naram Sin, ancient China could trace its roots possibly as far as 11000 years or more. It must be said though, that prior to the formation of the Chinese 'nation proper' in the Oin Dynasty of 221 BC, Chinese civilisation was little more than a patchwork of independent states each ruled by its own king or tribal chief. Although there was a central king who held nominal power, and powerful hegemons sometimes holding and exercising considerable influence, each state remained to be ruled as an independent political entity with its own tribal customs, culture and more importantly, music. At a very early stage, the Chinese had discovered and developed the technology to create copper trumpets, bronze chimes and drums. Some of these being designed for worship others to be used in war.

The ancient Greeks some 2000 years ago, had also perfected the art of manufacturing trumpets from copper or bronze, as had the Romans at least 2000 years ago. However, the oldest use of trumpets fashioned from animal horns would appear to be attributed to Egypt, probably tracing their lineage back some 4000 years. Solid evidence of metal trumpets dating back at least 3000 years was established by the discovery of the silver and copper trumpets in the tomb of Tutankhamen.

The true origins of blown instruments such as ram's horns however are quite obscure, but certainly the Bible has an account of Joshua laying siege to the South Palestinian town of Jericho. In 1440 BC:

> And seven priests shall bear before the ark seven trumpets of rams' horns: and the seventh day ye shall compass the city seven times, and the priests shall blow with the

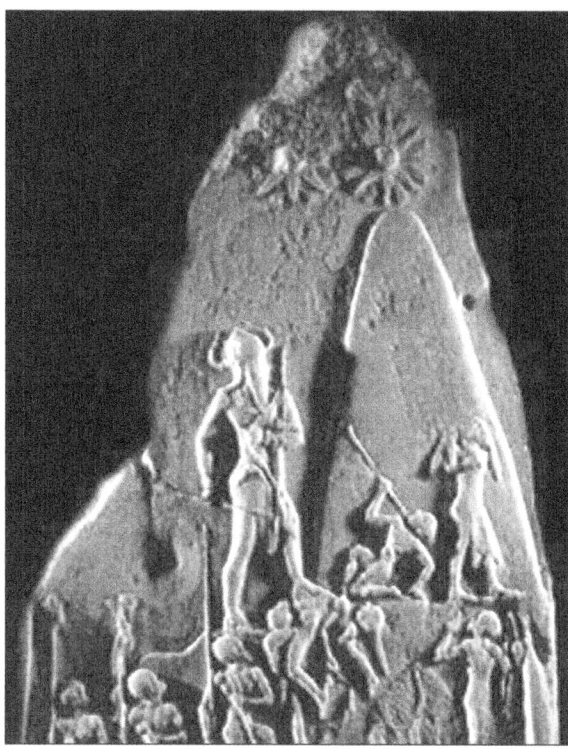

The Stele (monument) to Naram Sin showing the king towering over his enemies during a successful mountain campaign. The question remains is that a wounded soldier trying to remove an arrow from his throat or is it a trumpeter defiantly sounding to the last breath?

trumpets, and it shall come to pass, that when they make a long blast with the rams' horns and when ye hear the sound of the trumpet, all the people shall shout with a great shout; and the wall of the city shall fall down flat...and it came to pass, when the people heard the sound of the trumpet, and the people shouted with a great shout, that the walls fell down flat, so that the people went up into the city... and they took the city.

Subsequent archaeological digs have dated a settlement on the site of Jericho as far back as 7800 BC. Further excavations have indicated that in one period of 1000 years Jericho's walls had fallen and been repaired no fewer than 16 times and there was also evidence of several fiery destructions. None of these incidents however, could be attributed to the Israelites' actions. The important point to draw from this episode is that the Israelite troops were said to be led by their priests who were blowing rams horns. Thus it can be seen that, even amongst the earliest accounts of trumpeters (sic.) on the battlefield, it was clearly not a job delegated to the lower echelons.

The trumpet then, in one form or another, is believed to have been the original battlefield instrument: how far back into history this takes us is from the foregoing at least questionable. The fixing of a date for the invention and manufacture of a metal trumpet is impossible to establish without some hypothesis. Early in their history, the ancient

Sacred icons – clearly of Jewish origin being transported away from the sacked and destroyed Temple of Jerusalem following the Hebrew/Roman wars of AD70. Note – amongst these sacred items are two metal trumpets. (By kind permission of OUP.)

Egyptians had recognised the value of music. However, firm evidence of its instrumentation and extent was only made apparent from studies of the Pharaonic period – that is after 3100 BC. The metal trumpet in ancient Egypt probably traces its lineage, with reasonable certainty, back to the beginning of the New Kingdom (ca.1570 to 1070 BC) but it is believed by some historians that its existence as a foremost military instrument is likely to have been established somewhere in the span of the Old Kingdom (ca. 2686 to 2181 BC) – thus easily preceding Naram Sin by a considerable period of time.

The ancient Egyptians held all forms of music in high esteem, whether religious, popular or military in its application; their principal military instruments being the trumpet and the drum. Both these instruments were used on the march but for battlefield signalling and at court, the trumpet, with its bright incisive tone was the preferred instrument. There are many depictions of the Egyptian army in battle and on the march, from which it is possible to identify that the trumpeter's post was generally at the head of his division in the vanguard. The drummers however, were stationed at the centre of the formation and in proximity to the battle standard bearers, perhaps establishing at an early stage the link between drums and the colours, which continues to this day. There is also evidence from these representations, of trumpets and drums being formed en masse creating a band, being drawn up to one side with troops marching past much in the style of modern armies.

Music in general, was very much an everyday part of life in all ancient civilisations and musicians being largely professional men and women, were held in high esteem and were drawn from all walks of life; the highest in status being those who played in the temples and the palace, the latter being the most likely source of battlefield trumpeters. Lesser musicians, though still professional, would provide music for workshops and farms.

Instrumental groups such as percussion, wind and strings were all represented and used to one extent or another. Wind instruments included flutes, both end blown through a reed, like the Greek aulos, or side blown like the fife or transverse flute and of course the trumpet and the range of percussion instruments in vogue.

Amongst many other treasures of ancient Egypt, discovered in the tomb of Tutankhamen, were two trumpets; one of silver and one of copper. The silver trumpet, which is currently in the collection of the Egyptian Museum in Cairo, is 58 cm in length, the bell being 8.8cm wide and the tube between 1.7cm (near the mouth-piece) and 2.6cm (at the bell joint). It is made of beaten silver, with a thin gold band of decoration around the edge of the bell and at the mouthpiece end, both forged onto the silver. The conical tube and the bell were manufactured in two separate pieces and soldered together using pure silver. The bell of the trumpet is richly decorated and depicts, on one side, the gods Ptah (god of creation and rebirth), Amun (god of wind and ruler of the air) and Ra-Harakhty (Ra was the Egyptian sun god who was also often referred to as Ra-Harakhty, the creator of the world, who controlled the daily cycle, of sun rise and sun set each day, symbolising renewal) and on the other, a representation of the king.

Owing to its fragility, the original silver trumpet has been played only twice since its discovery. In the spring of 1939, a modern mouthpiece was inserted into this ancient instrument with the intention of recording its sound, but at the first attempt at sounding, the trumpet suffered some damage; fortunately it was able to be repaired immediately and subsequently managed to survive the eventual broadcast. During this recording the notes obtained by the military trumpeter employed were c, e, g and c', very similar to the harmonic series of the modern bugle.

China laid claim to the creation of ancient instruments in the form of drums, the existence of which was evidenced by the discovery of two drums near the Yellow River at Taosi which are said to be approximately 4000 years old. One of the drums was a metre high and fashioned from a hollowed out tree trunk. It displayed evidence of having been fitted with a skin head at one end and, like many Chinese drums, showed evidence of having been painted red. The other drum was crafted in clay rather like a wheel thrown pot, a style of design and manufacture which was very common in China. It too, showed evidence of having one end fitted with a skin membrane.

Bronze drums, also of Chinese origin dating back approximately 2000 years, have been unearthed in their hundreds in parts of China and Southern Asia. Drums in Chinese history were not only used for worship and sacred occasions but also, predictably like so many nations of the ancient world, at war. The Chinese, being an inventive race however, found in 400BC, a use for drums which exhibited the technical ingenuity and principles of a geophone (ground sensor). In the days of walled and fortified cities, it was current practice for besieging forces to dig tunnels under the walls of the fortifications; tunnels which could be used in a variety of ways such as simply tunnelling in to gain entry, or to tunnel under the strongest part of the walled fortification and either create a huge fire which dried out and weakened the supporting earth and foundations which would ultimately cause the walls to collapse or, if time was a critical factor, the tunnels could end in a chamber which could be filled with blasting powder to achieve the same ends but significantly quicker. In order to have some indication that tunnelling was in progress, the Chinese developed possibly the first early warning device by using drums. The drums used in this case being 200ltr clay pots with a highly tensioned skin membrane stretched across the top. Each drum was then placed and set up in a specially dug shaft approximately 15 feet deep and four feet wide. The positioning of the shafts was critical and was influenced greatly by the requirement to protect the most vulnerable portion of the walls or fortifications. This could only be successfully done following a detailed combat appreciation both within and without the walls, viewing the problem from the defence and attack positions. Once all drums were sited, the final preparation saw the placing of several small clay pellets or small pebbles on the highly tensioned membrane – thus any attempt at digging or tunnelling nearby would give rise to vibration of the surrounding earth and rock causing the pebbles on the nearest drum heads to move, creating an audible sound rather like a snare vibrating. If the drums had been sited accurately, the direction of attack might be determined and counter measures could be taken to defeat the tunnelling operations.

So, it might reasonably be assumed that the creation and use of the trumpet and the drum as military signalling instruments employed by the foregoing and other ancient civilisations, laid the foundations of their use, development and deployment for all other military organisations that followed.

2. Other Percussion Instruments

Other percussion instruments in ancient Egypt before the introduction of the drum, included small hand held tabors, rattles, castanets, bells, cymbals and a sophisticated form of rattle called the sistrum which was specifically used in religious ceremonies and worship. Hand clapping to provide rhythmic accompaniment was common, and vocally both male and female voices were used.

The drum proper for the purpose of this study is thought to have appeared in ancient Egypt during the period known as the Middle Kingdom, from c. 2040 – 1786 BC. Initially these drums were constructed by hollowing out a tree trunk and contouring the outer shell in the shape of a barrel. Skin heads were not in evidence, the drum player beating instead on the side of the drum, the hollowed body of which would act as a resonator amplifying the sound. These cumbersome and weighty instruments nonetheless gained favour in military usage. On the march these instruments would have been carried on some form of sling or harness thus permitting the drum player the use of both hands to beat out a marching rhythm. For long or arduous marches over rough or difficult terrain an alternative means of carriage might include a two man team, where one had the drum slung on a harness and carried on his back the other marching immediately behind beating the drum. In time, more elaborate drums were to evolve, introduced from the Palestinian region in c.1750 BC. Shaped like a goblet or wheel thrown pot, they had a skin batter head and open bottom end.

The later appearance, in the New Kingdom (Ca 1570 to 1070 BC) of a cylindrical drum with a skin head tightened by means of cordage across a wooden hoop, caused other forms of military percussion instruments to gradually fall from favour, especially amongst the infantry whose drummers must have been delighted with the new, lighter more resonant and responsive drum.

Whilst the trumpet and drum were firmly established, both in civil ceremonies and for military purposes, the later military employment of these instruments in ancient Egypt was, for eons fairly superficial. Despite its wealth and sophistication, ancient Egypt held no particular ambitions to invade and conquer or to harbour illusions of creating a great empire. It was considered to be the most peace loving country of the ancient world.

Ancient Egyptians thought of their land as two separate types. Black land, which was the fertile strip of land adjacent to the Nile, whose flood plains received an annual layer of black silt during each flood season and Red land, being the wide harsh and barren desert region which, along with the Nile on the Eastern boundary, created natural anti invasion barriers. As a consequence of this safe homeland ideology, ancient Egypt saw no necessity for the need to raise and sustain a professional standing army: that was until the invasion of the Hyksos in about 1720 -1710.BC. Josephus Flaviius, a historian of the first century BC, described the account of the conquest and occupation of Egypt by the Hyksos, taken from contemporary writings of the time.

> By main force they easily seized it (Egypt) without striking a blow; and having overpowered the rulers of the land, they then burned our cities ruthlessly, razed to the ground the temples of gods ... Finally, they appointed as king one of their number whose name was Salitis.

Some latter day historians consider this account to be incorrect and that there was no invasion by military might but rather more of a creeping occupation of the Egyptian fertile lands by Hyksos settlers which eventually led to a coup d'etat and the seizing of control of government by the Hyksos. This idea gathers some credence by way of the wording of the first line "...without striking a blow..." either way, the Egyptians were subjugated and their lands occupied.

Prior to the arrival of the Hyksos, ancient Egypt had a loosely organised part time army, equipped only with elementary weapons. It did however have a corps of full time regulars whose normal tasking embraced palace guard duties and acting as border police. In times of need, conscripts were drawn from the farmers and peasants of the land, cobbled together in makeshift units and led, inevitably, by noblemen. Whilst this was adequate to set down any bush fire incidents or minor civil unrest, clearly such a force was no match for a determined invader.

Subsequent to the Hyksos invasion, the Egyptians noted that the weaponry used by their invaders was, by comparison to the Egyptian weapons, vastly superior, e.g. instead of soft iron arrowheads, the Hyksos had theirs manufactured from sharpened bronze alloy. Alloys being lighter and harder than pure metals this improved the range, velocity and ultimately, penetration of bow-launched missiles. This technically improved arrow's range and velocity was further enhanced by the use of compound bows whose wings were built from laminated sections of differing types of wood and bone thereby improving launch potential. For protection, light but strong wooden shields – covered in bull hide and studded with metal nails were the order of the day. Above all else was the two-wheeled chariot – the early form of 'main battle tank'. So effectively did the Egyptians adopt and adapt these items of offensive equipment that they eventually ousted the Hyksos. Egypt now raised, trained and sustained a fully professional army and, by the middle of the18th Dynasty (c. 1539 – 1295 BC) had become something of a major military power, expanding its influence to create its own empire in the region – with which came the resultant increase in and sophistication of the use of battlefield signalling instruments and the selection and training of military trumpeters and drummers; positions of some importance.

3. Other Influences on Military Music

Paradoxically, in spite of the professional status of musicians in ancient Egypt, little in the way of written notation exists prior to the Graeco-Roman period, which ran from ca 331 BC to AD 395. Clearly, no great civilisation such as ancient Egypt ends overnight; there must be a form of gradual transition from one state of being to another. So it was for the Egyptians, approximately the last third of their existence being influenced by the bloody wars with their sworn enemy, the Hittites in the north and the future insurgencies of the Persians, Greeks and the Romans amongst others.

Egypt, post-Hyksos, was now free and able, for a while anyway, to enjoy a period of independence, however, in 351 BC Persia, seeking to fulfil its imperial ambitions, made its first, unsuccessful, attempt to invade Egypt but was repelled. A second attempt was made in 342 BC, this time with success. Persian vengeance though was dire; city walls were destroyed as a precursor to a reign of terror wherein temples were desecrated, looted and burned. The Persians, not surprisingly gained a significant amount of wealth from this episode – and to rub salt into the wound – crippling taxes were inflicted on the populace. These taxes were imposed partly to fund the Persians desire for opulent living and partly to weaken Egypt so that it could never rise up against them. For the 10 years that Persia controlled Egypt, religion was proscribed, sacred books were stolen or destroyed and the Egyptians in general were treated very badly.

Information regarding Persian music is somewhat scarce but what is certain is the existence of the Persian tabire (drum) and the karranay (trumpet), later named as the salpinx by the Greeks. Persian musical instruments also included the tanbur (lute) the nay (flute), chang (harp), rabab (viol), and the nay-i siyah (reedpipe).

Persian influence and domination of ancient Egypt and its environs was eventually terminated by a crushing defeat of its numerically superior army at Gaugamela.

In 335 BC Darius III had become the ruler of Persia and ergo of Egypt; that is until the arrival on the scene of one Alexander the Great of Macedonia who intended to increase his vast empire by claiming Egypt.

Picture the scene: the Persian army, under the command of King Darius III, (numbering approximately 200,000), faced a Macedonian (Greek) army, (numbering approximately 35,000) commanded by Alexander The Great – here, at Gaugamela the Persian army was about to meet its Waterloo; though not without a struggle. Out-thought and out-fought, Darius' army was deceived by the right wing of Alexander's cavalry, which moved off to the right but kept to a line of march which was parallel to the Persian front line, giving the impression that they were intending to effect a right flanking attack. Consequently, Darius began to deploy part of his formation to counter the threat to his left flank, thereby opening a gap in his army, into which the remaining Macedonian cavalry galloped, followed by the famed and feared 'Macedonian phalanx'. The phalanx consisted of a formed and disciplined body of men sixteen wide and sixteen deep each armed with a three metre pike. Whichever angle or style of attack chosen, the best that an opponent might achieve before being mortally injured or killed outright, or losing his horse to fall prey to a hacking demise from the inner ranks of men, was the incursion of three or four ranks depth into this bristling 'hedgehog' of lances. Positioning three or four phalanxes adjacent to one another would present a virtually impenetrable block of pikes and soldiers.

The clamour of battle during such an action would have been punctuated by blaring trumpet signals and the thunder of drums on both sides; to those having the upper hand, there would be signals to spur men on to greater glory, to those on the lesser side, frantic signals to try to recover a situation before it became completely untenable with the risk of being defeated in detail; which in spite of Darius' Goliath to Alexander's David and the urgent signalling from Persian trumpets and kettle drums – defeat was suffered. Shortly after the battle, Darius was assassinated by order of Bessus, one of his own noblemen.

Following the overthrow of the Persians, the ensuing Greek occupation of Egypt was well received, even to the extent of Alexander being made a Pharaoh by the Egyptians.

Apart from Egypt, Alexander's empire now included Greece, Thrace, Turkey, the Near East, Mesopotamia, and Asia extending all the way to India. No other empire of this magnitude had previously existed. The Egyptians considered Alexander as their liberator, freeing them from Persian oppression and were content to take him as their king. He built a magnificent city situated at the 'crossroads of the world' right on the Nile delta. In true conquering hero come liberator style, with great modesty, he named the new city, Alexandria.

So for the time being, Egypt is ruled by a Greek king; Alexander the Great has taken Egypt from the Persians, and made it a part of the Greek Empire. The arrival of the Greeks brought an unprecedented amount of change in Egypt, overlaying the existing society with facets of their own. The Greeks ruled successfully over Egypt by mingling Hellenic traditions with the legacy of the Pharaohs. The Greek kings, followed in the ancient Egyptian tradition of having themselves deified as gods, having temples built, and having statues made in their honour. Many of the statues, reliefs, and funerary objects which are today, in museums around the world, are from this era.

Eventually, following a bout of fever (probably malaria) in June 323 BC, Alexander died and the Greek royal line was replaced by the Ptolemaic dynasties, the last Pharaoh of which was to be the redoubtable Cleopatra, who as a result of her decision to support Mark Anthony in one of many internecine power struggles, found herself to be on the wrong side. Mark Anthony lost both the political and military battles with Rome and as a result, committed suicide. Rather than suffer the humiliation of losing her kingdom and be afforded the gory fate that would be hers, she too committed suicide. Legend has it that she held an asp (venomous snake) to her breast and caused it to bite her, with obvious consequences. She died on August 12th 30 BC at the age of 39 but since Egyptian religion declared that death by snakebite would secure immortality, she achieved her dying wish, never to be forgotten. Her death marked the end of the Egyptian monarchs. The Romans came in to rule in Egypt as part of their empire.

Rome's rule over Egypt officially began with the arrival of Augustus in 30 BC. He depoliticised the country and neutralised any rivalries for its control amongst other powerful Romans. For almost a decade, Egypt was garrisoned with Roman legions and auxiliary units until conditions became stable.

Egypt then, became a part of the Roman Empire, being named by the Romans as simply 'Ægyptus Province'. This province (or satrapy) was governed by a Prefect (or Satrap), drawn not from the Senate (to avoid any unnecessary political interference) but from the Equestrian (upper middle class) strata and nominated by the Emperor. Very sensibly, the Prefect, recognising that Rome's main interest in the Ægytus Province was to provide a reliable supply of grain to the city of Rome, replaced only the highest ranking Greek officers, leaving in place all other administrative officers and scribes, (embracing the old adage – if it ain't broke don't fix it!) Greek remained the language of government influenced only by those Romans in high office. Since the Romans did not settle in great numbers in Egypt, culture, education and more importantly music, remained largely unchanged, the Romans respecting Greek and Egyptian beliefs and customs. Inevitably though, some of the culture of the Roman state and empire was bound to make its mark.

Music formed a major part of both Greek and Roman cultures and it is certain that of the greatest influence in the Graeco-Roman era, one upon the other, Greek rather than Roman was the most profound, not only in Graeco-Roman Egypt but right up to the present day thanks to the likes of Pythagoras and other Greek thinkers, who conducted detailed studies of the science and theory of musical sounds leading to the establishment of a series of modal scales which have greatly influenced the scalic systems of major and minor keys in use in western music today.

4. Grecian Influence

It is clear that in ancient Greece and its empire, the study of music theory, writing and composing music as well as the ability to play a musical instrument, were rated so highly that it predated formal academic study. Anyone able to play a musical instrument was considered to be very valuable as a citizen, ranking alongside metalworkers and craftsmen as people of substance and culture. Usually, only the wealthier Greek families could aspire to music lessons for their offspring, thus creating social barriers excluding the less well off. Bear in mind the majority of ancient Greeks were subsistence farmers, eking a meagre existence from the land and or sea.

The most popular instruments for musical entertainment were the lyre, flute and timbrel (a kind of tambourine). At court and on the battlefield however, the brash tones of the trumpet as a martial instrument were used for fanfares and military signalling.

The continuing military use of the trumpet is established at a later date in the *Tactics of Ælian* (Ælianus Tacticus), a Greek military writer of the 2nd century AD who states;

> ... it is recommended that trumpeters be deployed at one to each company.

In fact, the Greeks attached such importance to the instrument, they were known to have conducted competitions in trumpet playing at the Games. When marching their soldiers from one location to another though, the Greeks used the flute. The trumpet was regarded as too brash and inspiring and likely to make the soldiers impetuous, therefore the flute was employed. This is borne out by the following quotation from Thucydides, reporting on the Peloponnesian War:

> The Spartans moved slowly, and to the music of many flute players, who played, not as an act of religion, but in order that the army might march evenly and in true measure, and that the line might not break.

Thucydides, a wealthy Athenian, was the first philosophical historian who recorded events exactly as they occurred, free from mythology and poetic licence. He had first-hand experience of Athenian and Spartan troops at war. At the start of hostilities in the Peleponnesian War in 431 BC he, in his own words, "had the leisure to observe affairs somewhat particularly" – then began to record events on a daily basis – an early version of the commanding officer's diary – in the belief that it would prove to be a "great and

THE ANCIENT WORLD 21

Young Greek aulos player – Many of these would be assembled into a 'corps' which would be positioned immediately behind the leading battle formations – literally to play the Hoplites to war.

memorable war above all others." Events justified his judgement, for the Pelopennesian War proved to be a twenty-seven year fight to the finish for the leadership of the Greek Empire between the two most powerful polis (city states) in Greece, Athens and Sparta. Not surprisingly, his account of the war ran to eight volumes over which he took enormous pains to be accurate and totally impartial. This is mentioned simply to underwrite the validity of the above quotation, thus verifying the Greek mode of marching their troops to the sound of the flute. The flute, more properly aulos – used in this regard was not a flute at all; the Greek name aulos, is almost always misinterpreted when translated into English. It was of a type that was end blown, like a recorder, but was in fact a double reed instrument in the style of the oboe, each body section having its own reed. The two body sections were of narrow conical bore, one being played by each hand. The pipes measured anything from twelve to twenty inches (35-50 cm) in length. It is clear from the quotation that many flute players would have been in evidence and would most likely have been massed as a 'corps' of flutes marching in rear of the leading fighting formations.

Unlike the ancient Egyptians, the ancient Greeks, in spite of their sophisticated and cultured lifestyle, were very much a warlike nation. Many able bodied Greek men went to war almost every year of their lives, not for territorial gain but to maintain their city state's political dominance and will over others. The Hoplite (foot soldier) was the mainstay of the Greek Army. He had to be wealthy enough to buy his own armour and weapons and was naturally, recruited from amongst the ranks of the middle classes. Clearly then if they were to be led on the march by flute players those flute players were required to be of equal standing or better.

The ancient world was not confined to Egypt, Greece or Rome. There is also evidence of the use of trumpets by others e.g. the Chinese, the Hebrews and many others. The Chinese created copper-alloy trumpets and bronze chimes 2,200 years ago, however, the prize for innovation appears to still rest with the Egyptians who introduced animal horn trumpets nearly 4,100 years ago.

From biblical evidence it seems that the Hebrews also used trumpets in religious ceremonies as well as rejoicings and war. The Book of Numbers in the Old Testament states that God commanded Moses to have two hasoserah or metal trumpets made; in this case made specifically of silver. Josephus describes them as being a narrow tube flaring out at the end with a broad bell, the whole being 40cm long. Having spent some 400 years under Egyptian bondage, it seems likely that the Hebrews would have been exposed to the sound of trumpets of all types and would, it is assumed, naturally have adopted them for their own military and religious needs. Such events as common assemblies, moving the Ark, swearing of oaths of allegiance, royal accession, the laying of a temple foundation stone and feast days would all have been graced by the presence of trumpets. In fact, the Feast of Trumpets still marks the beginning of the Jewish New Year and is observed during the month of Tishrei (September/October). In Hebrew, Feast of Trumpets is Rosh Ha-Shanah, Rosh meaning head and Shanah meaning year. According to tradition, this was the day when God created the world, though some suggest it was the day that Adam was made. Psalm 47 is read before the trumpet is blown; it is a call to all nations to acknowledge God as the Creator and King over all the earth:

With trumpets and sound of cornet make a joyful noise before the LORD, the King.

At the Feast of Trumpets the shofar is also blown to announce the New Year and to call the people to repentance. Apart from the above use of the trumpet, it was also used militarily, to assemble Hebrew warriors to battle against their enemies.

5. Roman Influence in Britain – Roman Brass Instruments

The expansion of the Roman Empire continued in the northern hemisphere with the invasions of Britain, firstly in 55-54 BC by Caesar, and again, rather more successfully, under the Emperor Claudius in AD 43. With them came a host of warlike instruments – mainly brass wind instruments. The most important of these was the tuba or straight trumpet. Made of copper or bronze, about four feet seven inches (120 cm) long and, for much of its length, having a fairly straight cylindrical bore, with a widely flared bell at the end. It was composed of three sections for ease of transit and to avoid damage, it was also fitted with a detachable mouthpiece. It was very similar to the Greek salpinx, the latter being of similar size, but with a tulip-shaped bell (sic.). Both types were reported as being played by the Greeks at the Games, where volume was considered above tone. The sounds described for competition purposes being – a long, drawn out tone to demonstrate breath control, a series of sharp, blasting tones, presumably at differing pitch to demonstrate embouchure strength and dynamics and a great warlike noise, presumably to create as much fear inspiring noise to demonstrate strength of embouchure, lip flexibility and staying power.

The cornu was the next most important brass instrument; undoubtedly the largest at ten feet six inches (320 cm) in length, even when curled for ease of transit and handling, it measured about four feet seven inches (140cm) in diameter. It too had a detachable mouthpiece which was about six inches (15cm) in length. Thought to be of Etruscan origin, it appears to trace its roots back to use as a hunting horn.

The lituus, was a variant of the tuba but curving upwards at the bell, rather in the style of the long, alpine horn. At two feet six inches (78cm) it was the smallest of the instruments and a specimen, recovered from the Rhine at Dusseldorf, displayed rings on the body for attaching a cord or strap.

Musicians using these instruments were called Æneatores but more specifically,

An excellent example of a carved relief located on Trajan's Column showing Roman soldiers carrying and playing cornu – noticeably the largest of the Roman brass instruments.

according to Grant's *The Army of the Caesars*, Æneatores were specified as either Tubicines, Bucinatores or Cornicines, according to which instrument they carried. All troops of Horse, every maniple (Roman division) and every century of Foot used either the tuba or cornu or sometimes both, being used for signals for every situation of battle. The lituus seems however, to have been mainly used by the cavalry.

The buccina, similar to the tuba, but broadening towards the open end rather in the shape of a straight, one pint beer glass, was principally used to conduct the movement of troops detached from the main body of the army, to mark the hours of the night for the night watchman; to sound reveille and other more mundane routine calls for meals, parades etc. The players of these instruments, it would appear, had fewer privileges than the other Æneatores and their duties also embraced acting as grave-diggers or wood-cutters.

Again from the historian Josephus, we find an account of a Roman detachment breaking camp and presumably reacting to trumpet calls sounded on the buccina:

> Now when they are to go out of their camp, the trumpet gives a sound, at which time nobody lies still, but at the first intimation they take down their tents, and all is made ready for their going out; then do the trumpets sound again, to order them to get ready for the march; then do they lay their baggage suddenly upon their mules, and other beasts of burden, and stand, as at the place of starting, ready to march; when also they set fire to their camp, and this they do because it will be easy to erect another

camp, and that it may not ever be of use to their enemies. Then do the trumpets give a sound for the third time that they are to go out, in order to excite those who are a little tardy, that so no one will be out of his rank when the army marches. Then does the crier stand at the generals right hand, and asks them thrice, in their own tongue, whether they be ready to go out to war or not? To which they reply as often, with a loud and cheerful voice, saying, "We are ready." And this they do almost before the question is asked of them: They do this as filled with a kind of martial fury, and at the same that they so cry out, they lift up their right hands also.

It seems likely that all of these instruments may have been used on the march too, since the depictions held on the Column of Antonius and on the Arch of Constantine show Æneatores marching at the head of their armies.

Although the Romans had drums and percussion instruments, as has been remarked earlier, drums tended not to feature significantly on the battlefield. From their experiences during the invasions of Britain previously mentioned, confronted by the warlike and barbaric Britons, the Romans could note that they too used only trumpets and horns as warlike instruments. The discovery of relics of Celtic instruments, similar to those of the Ancient Britons unearthed in Ireland, indicate them to have been of considerable size and having the mouthpiece at the side rather in the fashion of the African Ashantee war horns. Often, the Britons would presage their battles for hours with taunting songs and deafening howls accompanied by the blowing of horns and trumpets in great numbers.

One of the most ancient and fearsome of these horns was the 'carnyx'. This was an instrument thought to be mainly of Celtic origin, fashioned from beaten bronze, and formed into a kind of flattened 'Z' shape with the central part of the 'Z' being upright rather than angled. The instrument was held and blown in the upright position so that the sound was projected from more than three metres above the ground and, with its boar's head sound box, with moving tongue and jaw, was used as a visual as well as aural spectacle.

Three carnyxes embossed on the Gundestrup Cauldron (extreme right) discovered in a peat bog in Denmark and said to be dated between 200 BC and 300 AD and fashioned in pure silver.

Both Caesar and Claudius were reputed to have feared and respected it. The boar's head element of a carnyx was unearthed in a peat bog in Deskford, north-east Scotland in 1816. This instrument was once common throughout much of Europe, although only five fragments are known, of which Deskford is the finest. It appears to have flourished between 300BC and AD 200, and found widespread use in Britain, France, parts of Germany and eastwards to Romania, and beyond, carnyxes apparently being present at the attack on the Greek sanctuary at Delphi in 279 BC. They are also represented on a sculpture in India, proof of the far-flung connections of the Iron Age world.

Following the second and longest Roman occupation of AD 43, the tribal leader, King, Prasutagus of the Celtic Icini tribe, bequeathed the tribe's lands and wealth to be shared between the King's two daughters and the Roman Emperor, in return for which his people would be left in peace. Upon the death of the King, in AD 61, the Roman Governor in Britain, Suetonius Paulinus, seized all the Iceni lands and possessions. The Queen of the Icini, Boadicea, raised issue with Paulinus, whose only response was to have Boadicea stripped naked and publicly flogged. Worse, she was then forced to witness the violation and rape of her daughters by a gang of Roman slaves. Boadicea swore revenge. A tall, robust Amazon of a woman, with a fierce eye and harsh voice, she sported an impressive mane of fiery red hair which reached to her waist. The Iceni were incensed by the treatment meted out to their Queen and, accompanied by other nearby tribes, rose up in revolt. Between AD 61 and AD 63 Boadicea exacted bloody reprisals for the humiliation of herself and her daughters. Her campaign began with the sacking and slaughter of the Roman garrison at Colchester. Those who survived fled, like rats deserting a sinking ship, the resident Consul fleeing to far-away Gaul (France). This was then followed by similarly brutal raids on London and St Albans. There were several smaller actions which, in one case saw the complete destruction of a Roman unit whilst on the march. Oblivious to the ambush waiting for them, the Romans were taken completely by surprise as hundreds of howling Britons fell upon their unprotected flanks – all being slaughtered without mercy. Throughout this spell of rebellion, hundreds of Romans – soldiers, men, women and children – perished under Boadicea's sword. This period of bloody vengeance by Boadicea's army was not to last and in AD 63 at or near Nuneaton, Suetonius' Roman army of 10,000 soldiers triumphed over Boadicea's army of about 200,000. Suetonius had deployed his legionaries in close order, with their shields interlocked. To their flanks were units of cavalry and to their rear, thick woodland and scrub.

Boadicea deployed her warriors onto the battlefield in a broad formation. So confident of victory were they that the Britons arranged for their wagon train to assemble in a crescent formation to the rear, rather in the style of an arena. From this point their wives and children could watch the battle unfold and the slaying of the hated Romans.

Suetonius, addressing his legionaries is reported as saying:

Ignore the racket made by these savages. There are more women than men in their ranks. They are not soldiers – they're not even properly equipped. We've beaten them before and when they see our weapons and feel our spirit, they'll crack. Stick together. Throw the javelins, then push forward: knock them down with your shields and finish them off with your swords. Forget about booty. Just win and you'll have the lot.

Suitably blunt and to the point.

Boadicea led her army forward into the narrowing field in a full frontal attack. As the advance continued, they became channelled into a tightly packed mass by the narrowing field. At approximately forty yards, their advance was met by a volley of Roman javelins or pilum. The pilum, with its soft iron head, was designed to bend when it hit and penetrated a shield, causing it to be virtually impossible to remove; the enemy would thus be either encumbered with a heavy iron pila, or have to discard the shield and fight unprotected; very few if any of the Britons would have had any armour. At twenty yards, a second volley of javelins was discharged slowing the advance considerably.

With the Britons' advance faltering, Suetonius instructed his trumpeter to sound the command to adopt the 'Roman wedge' formation, creating a front line that had the shape somewhat like the teeth of a wood-saw. The Romans could continue to fight but the Britons, due the pressure exerted by the middle and rearmost of their huge army pushing forward, rather in the style of an uncontrolled surge seen at some football grounds and being totally unaware of the carnage being meted out to their front ranks, played right into Roman hands. Once the Roman cavalry had been deployed against the Britons flanks, losses quickly mounted. The Britons attempted a retreat, but their exit was blocked by the crescent created by their own wagons; they were completely destroyed. The Romans killed not only the warriors but also the women, children and even pack animals. It is estimated that some 80,000 Britons fell compared to only 400 Romans: this closed the lid on the rebellion. The Britons, brave and tenacious warriors that they were, despite the earlier bloodied Roman noses, were ultimately to prove no match for the disciplined and well-trained Roman legions.

It seems unlikely that the martial music of the Britons had specific sounds or commands, unlike that of the Romans, but neither appeared to use percussion instruments to any great extent; the predominant instrument clearly being the trumpet or horn in one or other of its guises.

Further references to trumpets and war horns in use by the ancient Britons may be found in the several other documents: The ancient heroic epic poem 'Beowulf'- written in Old English alliterative verse, indicates:

They away hurried bitter and angry the minute they heard the war horn sing.

Later Anglo-Saxon manuscripts also indicate the use of the trumpet. An example of an ancient instrument from these times bears an inscription on its side which translates to:

When the trumpet ceases to sound, the sword is returned to its scabbard.

One line from the ancient ballad *Hardyknute* refers to:

That horn', quo' they, 'ne'er sounds in peace.

In the *History of Charles and Grymer – Swedish Kings* may be found the line:

All instantly fly to arms, and everyone prepares himself for battle; the trumpet sounds, and each warrior is accoutred.

Grose, in his book *Military Antiquities* (1801) indicates the discovery of several trumpets in England, said to be of Danish heritage, one of which was reported to be over five feet in length. There is also reference to the military use of the trumpet in the *Mosaic Ordinances* or *'Priests' Code* dating from the fifth century BC which states:

> And if ye go to war in your land against the enemy that oppresseth you, then ye shall blow an alarm with the trumpets; and ye shall be remembered before the LORD your God, and ye shall be saved from your enemies.

The concept of using trumpets and or horns as an adjunct of warfare appears to have been universal. But Britain, whose ancients' used trumpets or war horns, was to become significantly influenced by the Romans, whose own style had been influenced by the ancient Greeks, who in turn had been influenced, albeit to a lesser extent, by the ancient Egyptians.

The second, and more successful invasion and occupation of Britain by Rome, was to continue until AD 410. A very long occupation, which changed the lifestyle and culture of the Britons to match more closely the lifestyle and culture of the Romans, with their advanced engineering skills, professional army and well-ordered judicial system, the influence of the Romans in Britain is still evident to this day. However, in its latter days the great ship of the Roman Empire was fast heading for the rocks. Those Romans in the furthest flung corners of it were eventually withdrawn and the Roman Empire crumbled bit by bit.

The legacy from this occupation, in terms of military musical instruments and their use was invaluable.

6. Post Romano-Britain, the Saxons and the Vikings

This liberation from Roman life however, did not leave the Britons in peace to enjoy the benefits obtained under the Roman occupation: for some time before the Romans finally withdrew from English soil, the Saxons had been carrying out nuisance raids. With the demise of the Roman garrisons and the disappearance of the Roman sea-going fleet, the way was now open to the Saxon hordes to invade Britain to loot, burn, pillage and slaughter almost at will. The name Saxon is a generic title for those peoples drawn from three quite separate tribal sources – the Jutes, from Jutland and the Frisian Islands; the Angles, from the Germany/Denmark border regions, and the Saxons, from Old Saxony – now known as Schleswig Holstein. Hostilities between the native Romano-Britons and the invading Saxons continued over many decades. Doubtless, battles would have been fought and to one extent or another, directed on both sides by war horns and trumpets. It is difficult to imagine that the influence of Rome and its armed occupation, with its trumpets as part of the war machine had not rubbed off on the Romano-Britons; even so, eventually the Britons were subjugated by the Saxons.

The tribal and cultural lifestyles of the three Saxon groups are perhaps evidenced by their occupation of separate parts of Britain: London, Kent, Sussex and Hampshire for the Jutes, Southern England and the West Country for the Saxons and the Midlands and North of England for the Angles. Collectively the Germanic settlers of Britain, mostly Saxons, Angles and Jutes, along with the remaining populace were fully integrated and eventually became known as the Anglo-Saxons.

Anglo-Saxon Britain was eventually and at last, to enjoy a period of relative calm until the arrival of the Vikings in AD 793. The Vikings, (a generic name for those warriors from Denmark, Sweden or Norway) sailed across the North Sea to invade the north-eastern coast near Lindisfarne. Here they sacked and burned the monastery, stole its treasures, murdered the monks and spread terror amongst the populace. Although terrible as it was, this was nothing more than one of many limited incursions which were to follow around the coasts of Britain over the next few years. In AD 865 a great army of Vikings invaded England, engendering open warfare between the Anglo-Saxons and the invaders.

The Viking raiders often came in under cover of the morning sea mists, their shallow-draft vessels slipping silently through the reeds of the river mouths to shallow, sandy beaches. The raiding party would then assemble and move covertly inland. Churches and monasteries were ideal targets due to their collections of silver and gold artefacts and the chance to take prisoners for slavery. This abundant source was soon depleted and the raiders' attention turned to the Anglo-Saxon farms and villages for food and horses. Eventually, the Viking raiders were to appear more frequently; so much so that they began to set up makeshift camps and stay over the winter months. Over time the raiders' camps became settlements to such an extent that at one time, most of England was under the Viking heel or Danelaw. All this warring must inevitably have been accompanied by the use of war horns and trumpets, but now the Anglo-Saxon influence had been enriched by the Viking style and usage.

By the year AD 1016, Cnut, King of Denmark, was asked to become King of England. He proved to be a wise king, spending much of his early reign settling the affairs and calming the fears of those parts of the kingdom worst hit by warring factions. Substantially, the reign of Cnut (or Canute) heralded the end of Viking military incursions into England, although sporadic raids around the coast continued for some time.

The last great feat of Scandinavian arms in England was in 1066, when King Harold Godwinsson, then newly crowned king, defeated the army of Harald Hardrada, King of Norway, at the battle of Stamford Bridge near York. In doing so, Harold Godwinsson delivered a decisive victory, thereby breaking the power of the Vikings to wage overseas war. It was to be the final Viking raid.

7. 1066 and Onwards – the Norman Conquest

William, the Sixth Duke of Normandy, was a descendant of Rolf or Rollo, the first Duke and was clearly imbued with many of his Viking ancestors' qualities. Inheriting the Duchy of Normandy when but a boy, by the age of twenty four he had demonstrated sufficient strength of character not only to survive but to establish and exert his authority over his rebellious nobles, and by so doing, had become one of the most powerful rulers within the Kingdom of France. William's ambitions though went further. Across the Channel reigned his father's cousin, the childless Edward the Confessor, from whom it is said William obtained a promise that he should succeed Edward to the throne of England. When Edward died in 1066, William claimed his right to the English throne. However, Earl Harold, son of Godwin, who is also alleged to have promised William the throne, was chosen as king by the English. Upon Harold's acceptance of the crown, William prepared a large invasion force with the intention of taking England and its throne by right.

William's army sailed from the estuary of the River Dive to land, unopposed, at Pevensey Bay on the Sussex coast. Messengers were rapidly dispatched from Sussex to the north of England to warn Harold, who with his Saxon army, was still embroiled in a battle to retake Stamford Bridge and York from the last of a dwindling force of Viking marauders. Having accomplished this task, Harold marched his troops south as fast as possible, stopping only in London to gather reinforcements, by which time, William had extended his bridgehead and was ideally placed to resist attack. Harold though, a seasoned campaigner and astute general, had no intention of beginning this battle on the back foot. Upon his arrival in Sussex, he took up a strong defensive position on Calbec Hill, part of the Senlac ridge, a few miles north of Hastings. This put the English army in a very strong position, as the ridge had deep ravines, streams and marshy ground on either side. Harold had effectively blocked William's only route out of the Hastings peninsula, forcing him carry the fight to the English by means of a full frontal attack.

By positioning his army at the top of the hill, Harold had excellent visual command of the forward area and to the flanks. For the Normans it was going to be a real test of stamina, pitted against this experienced and confident army. For William's men, it was going to be an uphill struggle – literally! Harold built a wall of overlapping Saxon shields, (much in the style of the Roman legions). This wall extended across the entire front and was probably several ranks deep – a formidable defence. The front rank was usually made up entirely of the most skilled and courageous of Harold's troops, such as the Housecarls and Theigns. Further deployment of these regular troops throughout the body of the army, interspersed amongst the relatively less well armed and less able Fyrdmen or peasant soldiers, was done in order to stiffen the latter's resolve when engaged in battle.

Harold, quite rightly expected the wall to hold firm against assault and for William's men to tire and weaken from having to attack uphill. This, when adjudged to be the right time, would allow Harold's army to launch a counter-attack with relatively fresh troops strong enough to defeat the Norman invaders.

William, who had been surprised by the tremendous speed of Harold's advance from Stamford Bridge in the north, was, nonetheless in command of a disciplined and structured army. His army was divided into three contingents, each with its own commander. The left flank was comprised mainly of Bretons; in the centre, were the Normans under William's direct command; the right was a mix of French and Flemish troops. The order of battle for each of the contingents was uniform, being comprised of three divisions; the forward division was composed of archers, the second division infantry, and the rear, cavalry. William's plan was to use the archers first to send their arrows into the English ranks, to destabilise the enemy and cause maximum casualties from a safe distance. The infantry then would advance, under cover of this 'barrage' – engaging at close quarters with the enemy in hand-to-hand combat. Once the enemy lines had been breached, the cavalry would be dispatched to attack from the flanks and rear, using their speed and height advantage, to deliver the coup de grâce by slaughtering the fleeing foot soldiers. The effect of such a three-tiered escalation of might was designed to demoralise and break the opposing force.

At about 9.30am, on the morning of 14th October 1066, hostilities opened in a most peculiar fashion; William's personal court minstrel, Taillefer (Latin Incisor-ferri, meaning the 'Iron Cutter') rode out in front of the Norman force and paraded up and down before the English army reciting the *Chanson de Roland*, all the while hurling his sword skywards in a glittering arc and catching it by the hilt. An English soldier, tired of this arrogant display, ran out to challenge him and was instantly slain by the Iron Cutter's Sword. Taillefer, overcome with passion, then charged the English lines and was engulfed and killed. The 'Battle of Hastings', as it was to become known, began. Predictably, it was William's archers who opened hostilities sending a withering blizzard of arrows into the English ranks. William followed up his plan with an attack by the infantry and then possibly by the cavalry. Variations on this tactical theme continued throughout the day but the Saxon shield wall held firm. Tired and dispirited, William's army was in danger of collapsing completely. This low ebb of morale was brought to a head when in the early afternoon a rumour that William had been slain spread like wildfire through the Norman ranks. William, afraid that his troops might flee the battlefield, rode out in front of his soldiers and removed his helmet. With scant regard for his safety, rode up and down the ranks encouraging his troops to persevere. Thus by courage and leadership, William had pulled his army back from the jaws of defeat.

Once more the fight was engaged and again, the Normans were repelled. William withdrew and regrouped. Both sides by now were very tired, each having suffered casualties, especially the Norman infantry, having been exposed to the scythingly efficient and deadly Anglo-Saxon battle-axe. At this juncture in the battle, William spotted what might be a flaw in the otherwise disciplined and stoic English army's defence. The Bretons on the left flank, having been yet again beaten off by the English, began to retreat in some disorder down the hill. Seeing this, and greatly buoyed by their success hitherto, part of the English army broke ranks and pursued the retreating Bretons. Harold moved quickly to recover his troops and secure his right flank. For William, this represented an opportunity to be exploited. (It should be noted here that historians remain divided regarding the following account of the Norman tactics employed, some dismissing the 'feint' theory others supporting it but nonetheless whichever version one reads and supports, it makes for a good read.) For the next attack, William ordered the archers to fire all their remaining arrows high into the air for the final assault so that they fell into the rear ranks of the English army to cause maximum casualties. He further ordered the Breton division to feign retreat to cause the English to break ranks in pursuit. This indeed is what may have happened; seeing the whole Breton division apparently in headlong flight, Harold's army was drawn right into the trap. By the time the English soldiers had realised what was happening, it was too late. Suddenly confronted by a far from routed Breton division and under attack from the flanks and rear by cavalry, the end was inevitable. The rain of arrows falling from the sky caused very high casualties, including Harold who, it is said, was shot in the eye. With their King mortally wounded and the shield wall broken, the way was open – the Normans penetrated the English ranks, killing the fallen King and hacking his body into pieces. The morale of the English troops was shattered by the death of their leader, the battle ended in total defeat for the English, although the Housecarls and Theigns continued to fight to the death, but the outcome was never in doubt.

It is clear that, in order to exercise effective command and control over his archers, infantry and cavalry, William required a structured and easily understood series of signals if the battle was not to descend into chaos. These signals would have been delivered by the trumpeters at critical points in the battle to indicate for example 'Infantry Advance', 'Infantry Hold Ground', 'Cavalry Advance' or 'Cavalry Charge'. Whilst this was fine for controlling one's own troops, as with all such modes of signalling it was hardly covert in its application since the enemy force could also hear the signals and to a greater or lesser extent, be forewarned of the style and manner of the attack being launched. Nonetheless, the Normans had triumphed.

That the Normans had trumpets and other musical instruments is not in doubt, since as they sailed in to begin the initial beach landings, the Norman ships were said to resound with music, the army being accompanied by a great number of minstrels. Chronicles of the Battle of Hastings record the use of boisins and horns by the Normans. The boisin, said to be a name derived from the Roman buccina, was a large crooked trumpet. The word minstrel also came from the Normans and was used to describe those who practiced the musical profession.

The English army for their part used war horns. Little is known of their signalling procedures but it must be safe to surmise that it is unlikely to have been anything more than simple calls to 'Reverse Shields,' to face attacks from the rear, or 'Open Shields' to allow the axe wielding Housecarls and Theigns to deal out mortal strikes. Mainly it is thought their use was to provide belligerent noise production to un-nerve the opposition.

Over the following months, William captured Canterbury, Winchester and London. He was crowned King on Christmas Day 1066. William had conquered! The Norman influence of martial signalling now being added to the melting pot of military battlefield instruments and their use. Perhaps more significantly, this was the last time that Britain was to be successfully invaded.

Part II

From the Waytes to Cromwell

8. Elevated Status – Privileges and Pecking Order

It has then, it is hoped, been established that whenever they went into battle, kings and nobles were accompanied by their retinue of minstrels and trumpeters as indicated by Kappey in his book *Military Music*:

> The trumpet, with its bright and incisive tone, was annexed exclusively for the use of kings and nobles.

It was upon these trumpeters then that the king or noble commander relied in order to direct military movement by the use of predetermined signals. As members of the royal entourage, they held positions of some privilege and importance, holding equivalent status to officers, wearing the feathers of nobility in their caps and being provided with horses and grooms. There are many incidences in early English history where trumpeters, drummers and fifers marched at the head of the king's army. For example, it is said that Edward III was attended by a great number of trumpeters and drummers when he made his triumphal entry into Calais on the 4th August 1347, at the successful conclusion of a siege which had lasted eleven months. Later, in the reign of Henry VIII, drummers and viffleurs (fifers) are cited as marching at the head of the army during the siege of Boulogne in 1544. Although in a different context, at the coronation of James II in 1685, which was a lavish affair, the coronation procession had trumpeters, kettle drummers and the four drummers to the royal household lead by a fifer displaying a bannerol on his fife. In May 1910, for the state funeral of Edward VII, seventy-five drummers were used to play a specially written drum introduction to each of the funeral marches of Handel, Beethoven and Chopin. The drum piece consisted of a series of crescendo – diminuendo rolls punctuated by bass drum beats. This was reported in *The Graphic* newspaper as giving:

> ... the suggestion of the firing of musketry and the booming of artillery over the grave of a hero ...

Minstrels, drummers and fife players not surprisingly did not operate for free; in the records of public expenditure in the fifth year of the reign of King Edward I in 1276, there is to be found the mention of payment to one Robert, styled King of Minstrels, apparently for military service. In the year of 1292, similar entries are to be found of one Randolph – King's Trumpeter – who had also it seems, held such a position to Henry III. In 1310, an entry for one Roger, the trumpeter, a King's Minstrel and Janino le Nakerer (kettle drummer) shows them to have been paid 60 shillings, a very handsome sum for those days. The minstrels of Henry III comprised five trumpeters, two clarions, five pipers, three waytes and four others. They were recorded as having appointments for life by 'letters patent' and were remunerated at the rate of seven pence halfpenny per day. Additional rewards were

A copy of the percussion parts which served as an introduction to the funeral marches of Beethoven, Chopin and Handel – beaten by 75 massed drums and bass drums for the Funeral of Edward VII on 24th May 1910.

given, such as the payment in 1359 to the King's Herald and his companions the minstrels, of forty pounds for attending the tournament at Smithfield.

Henry V had seventeen minstrels, ten of whom were trumpeters. They accompanied him with all his martial train to France where they undoubtedly played their part in England's glorious victory at Agincourt.

A brief fast forward to the 17th Century reveals much about the importance of drummers and their ability to command a presence. When not being paid for additional services under the crown, drummers from the Foot Guards and Chelsea Hospital would supplement their regular income by attending the weddings of the wealthy to provide a touch of pageantry by forming a guard of honour and drumming a point of war to welcome the happy couple to a new life. More often than not, these drummer escorts were un-invited, the drummers having discovered the time and place of the event, pitched up, did their duty (sic) and having taken their repast, pinned the groom down to exact payment. This practice is listed in Francis Grose's *The Vulgar Tongue* (1785) as 'Cropping Drums'.

Now back to the 1300s… by the fourteenth century there were several grades of minstrel with a clearly established pecking order. First and foremost were those, as mentioned above, who were in the king's service. This embraced the court minstrels, drummers, fifers and trumpeters, all of whom would be clad in the royal livery. Closely aligned to the King's Minstrels were those employed by the nobility, both groups of musicians being seen as the 'aristocrats' of music at that time. Next came those who could wear the king's livery but were not actually in the king's pay. These musicians were granted the privilege of wearing the king's livery by what would today be termed as 'passing an audition' to test their musical competence. These musicians too were held in the highest esteem. The City of London also boasted a collection of musicians, the highest level being those who were freemen of the

From a work by Francis Sandford – The History of the Coronation of James II – This woodcut of the Coronation procession of James II in 1685 shows the four drummers of the Royal household lead by a fife player whose fife is decked with a bannerol.

various guilds and societies making up much of the wealth of the City and being granted the privilege of wearing the livery or badge of the guild to which they belonged. Being largely self-employed and having to earn a living by their own skills, the grant of wearing the livery gave them greater social status and offered a guarantee of integrity.

Next in the pecking order, came the lone, wandering minstrels who were largely part time or freelance. The relative size of London afforded them reasonable opportunities to scrape a living or improve income to augment that of the day job. Having a harp or lute and a dozen or so songs, these musicians extended their repertoire with sleight of hand conjuring tricks or juggling; the fitter ones performing acrobatics or tumbling. Not being overly particular as to the means by which they made a living, the wandering minstrel (or street busker in modern vocabulary) realised that the benefits gained by obtaining a livery cloak and badge, whether entitled to have it or not, would avoid his being hounded or harassed. Furthermore, it greatly improved his 'perceived' social status and ergo his chances of survival. Aldermen of the City were perplexed as to how the 'policing' of these wandering minstrels could be effected as very often the livery cloak and badge worn would be genuine but from a City company unconnected to music and since the playing of musical instrument was not an offence, little could be done. However, change was on its way.

These wandering minstrels were despised by the 'proper' musicians since the musical ability to play or sing to a credible standard, was oft times wanting. The very act of performing in the streets and/or ale houses and passing the hat round – was seen as lowering the tone of the art and science of music. Eventually in 1642, the passing of an Act of Parliament was made in which it was stated:

> ... If any person or persons, commonly called fiddlers or minstrels, shall be taken playing and fiddling, or making music, in any inn, alehouse or tavern, every such

person or persons shall be adjudged rogues, vagabonds, and sturdy beggars and be punished as such.

Initially, lower down the pecking order came the City Waits or Waytes. The Waits were to become the official City musicians, be paid a regular (though not large) wage and upon retirement, each man would receive a pension. Originally though, employed as nothing more than night watchmen to secure such as royal palaces, castles, camps or walled cities, their duties included calling the hours of the night, signalling the relief of posted sentries, fire watching or to sound the alarm in case of attack or infiltration by an enemy, this alarm to be sounded by horn or trumpet. It was this ability to sound signals on the horn which led to the development of City Waits becoming musicians proper. As musical instruments improved, the Waits received and learned to play, shawms, cornets, sackbuts and trumpets. Other more sophisticated instruments were to follow and, the Waits, having plenty of time for practice, kept pace with developments and a corps of musicians was born.

In the City of London, all Waits were Freemen, being granted the privilege of wearing the Livery of the City and a valuable silver badge and chain of office. Mention of City of London Waits is to be found in the City Letter Books as far back as 1334 but sadly, no detail is to be found of their exact duties. The first Waits were appointed to the City of London by Henry III ca. 1253. By the fifteenth century, waits were being primarily engaged as musicians and watch-keeping remained very much a secondary role. With these new skills came a widening of their duties and rather than sounding the horn to awaken folk from their slumbers, a small group of Waits would gather at the doors of the most senior persons and waft them from the arms of Morpheus by playing soft music. Apart from musicians of the Royal Household, the Waits were the only musicians permitted to play secular music and to be permitted to play for all City functions, both Royal and Civic and other special or festive occasions. Clearly, the Waits had moved up the pecking order to a position of some importance. Waits played an important role in the ceremonial life of the City, the old Marching Watch being a cross between the Lord Mayor's Show and a smaller version of the May Day Parade in Moscow to display the military might and facility of the City. The Waits took pride of place in these processions being placed second only to the Lord Mayor who was to lead the van. Next came the other city officials, grave persons, ensigns, players and Morris Dancers et al. Close behind them came a mass of thirteen fifes and twenty-five side drums. Thus can be demonstrated the importance of musicians both at Court and by definition, at war and that of the Waits of the City.

In the history of the Worshipful Company of Musicians, can be found the designation of 'waytes' – indicating the word to be derived from the Anglo-Saxon title of 'Wacian' meaning one who's task it was to wake, watch or guard.

9. Influence of the Crusades on English Martial Instruments

It is fairly certain, even from very early times, that for some armies, trumpets used in battle had developed distinct calls related to specific manoeuvres. According to Grant's *The Army of the Caesars*:

> The Trompetters doe call the souldiers to battayle and againe doe call them back by blowing a retraite ... 'as often as these may blowe, not only souldiers, but also standereds are ready at the sounding of them to be remove.

> ... in the fighte the souldiers might more easily obeye; if the captaines should command them, either to fight or to staye, to pursue or to retire.

Other early English manuscripts seem to indicate that this was not necessarily the case for all armies. For example – concerning the Crusade of Richard I – it is thought that movement was conducted to coincide with previously issued orders, the trumpets merely being the activator. This is perhaps borne out by the chronicle of one Geoffrey de Vinsauf who recorded:

> It has been resolved by common consent that the sounding of six trumpets in different parts of the armie should be a signal for a charge.

By and large then, it would seem that, with few exceptions, trumpets, in whatever form, were for many great armies, spanning thousands of years, the primary instruments of martial music. This applied equally in Britain, until the Crusaders returned from the East with newer and more exciting ideas.

The phrase 'it is almost certain that military music had not assumed any definite shape in Britain until after the time of the Crusades' is perhaps a little vague. From 1095 until ca. 1500, there were scores of military operations conducted by those who sought the material and holy privileges associated with the 'Wars of the Cross.' Paradoxically, only a few campaigns, mainly those that were pitched against Muslim-held objectives in and around Syria, Palestine and the eastern Mediterranean, are numbered and documented in detail. The Crusade initiated in response to an appeal by Pope Urban II in 1095 to re-capture the holy city of Jerusalem and release Eastern Christians from oppression, was subsequently to become known as the First Crusade. The next sizeable feat of arms mounted by the Crusaders in 1145, was nominated as the Second Crusade – thus any Crusader military actions carried out between 1095 and 1145, of which here were many were largely discounted. The numbering of subsequent Crusades followed the same pattern where lesser campaigns became overlooked in favour of the campaigns mounted by greater armies. Some differences of opinion still exist between scholars and historians where some believe there to have been eight or even nine Crusades. Certainly by the early 18th Century it was considered that there were only five Crusades – a number held by most modern historians and polemicists as correct today.

For the purposes of this book, the Crusade which is of the greatest significance to the adoption and use of musical instruments as an adjunct to war in England, is the third Crusade of 1188-92 , led by the English King Richard I (Richard 'Couer de Lion'). It seems likely that during and following this four-year campaign, the military use of musical instruments was initiated in a more orchestrated form in England.

The Crusaders learned that Saracen army minstrels were used primarily to indicate a rallying point. Under normal circumstances, the standards were sufficient to indicate the location of the command centre. However, in the turmoil of battle, the standards might become obscured and it was Saracen practice to group the minstrels around the standards and for them to blow and beat strenuously, without let during the action; any silencing of the clamour being an indication that the standards were in danger or indeed might have fallen. This musical display also served another purpose, namely to excite the spirit and courage, for the more violent the clamour, the more bold the soldiers became for the fray.

Musical instruments employed by the Saracens were said to include trumpets, clarions, horns, pipes, drums and cymbals, a fearful array causing a fearful racket. The Crusaders, not used to this shattering sound delivered in such a concerted manner, must at first have been confused or even frightened by this action. Soon, however, they came to see the value of such instruments as an adjunct to war and lost little time in adopting or adapting them to their own advantage. In particular the Saracen tabor (side drum) and the kettle-drum (naker or nakereth – from the Arabic naghghāreh) took the fancy of the Crusaders. Thus of necessity, it became the custom to recruit and train drummers to augment the other minstrels and trumpeters attached to the suites of kings and nobles.

10. A New Order – Foundations of a Standing Army

Until the early 1500s musicians, drummers, fifers and minstrels had belonged only to the suites of kings and high-ranking nobles. All this was about to change. In 1507, a meeting of the Diet – a Feudal Parliament – was convened in the German City of Worms. This meeting was to become probably the most significant event in the history of drums and fifes in all European armies.

Present at the time was one Georg von Frundsberg, leader of the powerful German Landsknecht mercenaries, modelled on the Swiss mercenaries' structure. He made a representation to the Diet requesting the Landsknechts be regularised and that they should have, as part of their establishment, drummers and fifers. It was agreed by the Diet that each Landsknecht company should be given " ... zwei Trommelschlager und zwei Pfyffer ... " – two drum beaters and two fifers." A Landsknecht regiment might consist of up to ten companies each comprising 100 trained and experienced troops and 400 recruits. Additionally, it was agreed that the colonel commanding a ten company Landsknecht regiment could have, as part of his personal staff, one Staff Drummer (Stabstrommler) and one Staff Fifer (Stabspfyffer) – thus making a total of twenty-one drummers and twenty-one fifers for signalling on the battlefield.

The allocation of a drummer and fifer to the colonel's staff implies the possible origins of the posts of Drum Major and Fife Major. Clearly, if they were selected to serve the regiment in a staff appointment, they were obliged to be roundly competent in their musical duties, the bulk of which would be the coordination and conduct of training for the other drums and fifes of the regiment in all aspects of field signalling to the satisfaction of the commanding officer.

It was Henry VIII who, having sheltered within the midst of a hired Landsknecht Regiment's *Igel* or hedgehog of pikes at the Battle of the Spurs in 1513, realised the value of the Landsknecht's massed drums and fifes next to him, beating out orders and battle signals. His presence there was confirmed and recorded by a French eyewitness, the Chevalier Bayard, the account being published later in his *Histoire du bon Chevalier*.

Prior to 1513, no mention of fifers appears in the records of the establishment of the English companies. Detailed records of the 1513 campaign do still exist, at Kew, compiled by Henry's Almoner (none other than the redoubtable Cardinal Wolsey) but fifers do not feature. Thereafter however, a fifer and drummer appear on the rolls in all subsequent campaigns of Henry's reign. Thus it might reasonably be concluded that it was indeed Henry VIII, influenced by his experiences of the Swiss and German mercenaries with their massed drums and fifes, who was responsible for the concept of the establishment of a drummer and fifer to each English company. In spite of the Royal impetus, even by as late as 1521 it seems that the establishing of company drummers was still not fully in place.

Since court trumpeters had operated largely on horseback, it seemed logical for trumpets and the cumbersome kettle-drums to be allocated to regiments of cavalry.

The less cumbersome tabor or side drum, being seen as a sensible instrument for foot soldiers to inherit for conveying signals on the battlefield and in company with the bag-pipe, used by them when on the march. The Royal Artillery and some Dragoon Regiments though, retained the use of side drums until the mid 1800s.

Some schools of thought however were still of the opinion that, commanders of both cavalry and infantry should have and use trumpeters to announce commands during battle. This tardiness to adopt appropriate musical instruments was not confined to the English, as indicated by the Italian statesman Machiavelli, in his treatise *Dell'arte Della Guerra* (The Art of War) (1521) which explains, in detail, effective procedures for the acquisition, maintenance, and use of a military force, directing, most strongly, that the army of Lorenzo the Magnificent was to make use of trumpets, fifes and drums in directing their battles. He also stipulated therein that the infantry was to obey the drum and fife and the cavalry the trumpet. He was particular regarding the adoption of the fife in order to:

better regulate the stepping together of troops.

For marching troops, the side drum had previously been traditionally accompanied by the bag-pipe, an instrument widely in use in the Middle Ages in England, staying in use until as late as 1683 but clearly, from the early 1500s, the fife was in the ascendant. In fact the fife became so popular, both for military use and entertainment, that Henry VIII was obliged to send dispatches to Vienna to obtain supplies to meet demand, both of the instruments and those who could play them.

All this expansion of drums and fifes required properly trained musicians to operate with the various regiments of the army. However, finding musicians to play the fife proved almost as difficult as procuring them. One commanding officer wrote:

I could only hire two of them and these would only sign on for a month at a time.

Another wrote:

I could not get any to serve under four men's wages and even then were but easy players and very drunkards.

The rates of pay for these civilian drummers were the same as those of a sergeant, both receiving one shilling (5p) per day as opposed to the private soldier who was paid 8 pence (approximately 3p) per day. Considering what was expected of them it was no wonder that drummers and fifers were difficult to come by – here are the words of one Ralph Smythe, a writer on military subjects during the reign of Elizabeth I:

All Captains must have drums and fifes and men to use the same, who shall be faithful, secretive and ingenious, of able personage to use their instruments and office, of sundry languages: for oftentimes they be sent to parley with their enemies, to summon their forts or towns, to redeem or conduct prisoners, and diverse other messages, which of necessity requireth language. If such drums and fifes should fortune to fall into the hands of enemies, no gift nor force should cause them to disclose any secrets they know. They must oft practice their instruments, teach the company the sound of the march, alarm, approach, assault, battle, retreat, skirmish or any other calling that of necessity should be known. They must be obedient to the commandment of their captain and ensign, when as they shall command them to come, go or stand, or sound their retreat or other calling. Many things else belonge to their office, as in diverse places of this treatise shall be saide.

Another document of the 1600s entitled *Officers and Duties Belonging to a Foot Compagnie Through All Their Degrees, From Private Soldier to a Captaine as Followeth* sets out the routine duties of a drummer thus;

Every Company also ought to have two good Drummers, that knoweth how to beate a call, a slow, or a swift march well, a charge, a retreat, and a Reveille: He should also be a linguist, because oftentimes he may be sent unto the enemy for the ransoming of prisoners, his duty is coming to the campe or garison of an enemy, having his Generalls passe in his hat, to beat a call, till he is fetched in, and because he shall not discover the weakness of guards, works, or trenches, he is led blindfold, and so carried to the Commander, and place where his prisoners are, with whom after he hath ransomed them, he is to returne to the camp, or garrison.

In fact there was a plethora of writers in the 16th and 17th centuries proclaiming similar duties and responsibilities of drummers as originally set out by Smythe. Such writers as Thomas Stywood (1582), Richard Barnaby (1587), Giles Clayton (1591), Edward Davies (1619) and many others, all advocated the prescription of duties similar to those set out by Smythe – his manuscript being the earliest and most often quoted. Clearly plagiarism was rife in those days and as for the actual signals prescribed, there is almost unanimity by writers each to the other regarding the repertoire required of a drummer; i.e. The typical listings include A Call, A Troope, A March (Quick or Slow), A Preparative, A Battaile, A Retreat; all of which convey little in their titles alone, but fortunately there survives an explanation of each:

- A Call – Gather to hear a proclamation or to parade with their captain for briefing.
- A Troope – Fall in for roll call, shoulder arms, advance pikes, and to Troope (follow) after their officer to the rendezvous according to daily tasking.
- A March – Dress into open order with muskets and pikes at the shoulder and march at the rate beaten by the drummer who will be instructed to beat either a quick march or a slow march.
- A Preparative – Adopt the appropriate rank and file formation, prepare weapons ready for the skirmish.
- A Battaile (Charge) – Continue the advance to contact in skirmish lines, maintain formation and be ready to step into the gap left by a comrade going down under effective enemy fire – keep pushing forward.
- A Retreat – Conduct a withdrawal in contact in an orderly fashion to gain tactical advantage, or to carry out relief in contact or to draw the enemy into a tactically

advantageous position.

Some writers advocated the requirement for a Reveille and also an Alarm, neither of which requires explanation. In 1643, Thomas Fisher indicates in his book *Warlike Directions: or the Souldiers Practice*, the addition of a Gathering, which appears to be much like a Call previously mentioned and is possibly the nomenclature used for the Scotch duty. He also separates a Battaile (charge) into its two component parts that is, on the sounding of a Battaile, take formation for the advance to contact and once engaged with the enemy, at the sound of a Charge, keep pushing forward by using 'hand to hand' pike and musket drills. His interpretation of a Call is to have every one paraded in front of their commander to hear proclamations and to be forewarned regarding military laws which ought to be kept.

For the trumpeter there was a similar catalogue of duties and sounds to be mastered. In 1672 for example, amongst others, one Thomas Venn, in one of his publications entitled *Military and Maritime Discipline*, offers the following;

> A Trumpeter, ought to be a man skilful in all the sounds of the trumpet, distinctly; he ought to deliver all Embassies, etc. He ought to observe the enemies works, guards, and souldiers, that he may give a good account thereof at his return. and for the better performance thereof, he ought to be a man witty and subtle, and to manage it discreetly; he ought not in the least to disclose anything as may prejudice his own party; he must not fail to sound the hours commanded.

This in essence, is based on similar lines to the duties of a drummer set out by Ralph Smythe – albeit somewhat abridged. Venn also lists what were termed the 'Six Points of War' required of the trumpeter as follows:

- Buttesella – Saddle up and prepare to move
- Mounte Chevallo – Lead horses out and mount
- A Standart – Report to the colours or to one's officer at the appointed place
- Tucquet (A March) – Fall in and take formation to set out and follow the officer
- Carga carga (A Charge) – When sounded and, following the directions or example of the officer, the soldier is to "give proof of his valour in the speedy charging of his Enemie"
- Auquet (A Watch) – Sounded at night and in the morning to mount and dismount the Guards

He mentions in passing the Proclamation, Call and Summons as additional but in all, the list is very similar to those calls required of the drummer.

As previously intimated, the dispatch of a drummer to beat a parley and to stand a musket shot away from the enemy's ramparts was at best fraught with danger. There was however a code of conduct which held that, the targeting of a drummer sent to parley was not the done thing. One such incident, recorded in a publication of 1589, attributed to Anthony Wingfield, entitled *A True Copy of a Discourse; written by a gentleman employed in the late voyage of Spain and Portingale* offers the following account of the drummers lot as follows:

The same day, the General having planted his Ordenance readie to batter, caused the town to be summoned (sent a drummer to parley) they of the town shot at our drum: Immediately after that there was one hanged over the wall, and a parley desired, wherein they gave us to understand, that the man hanged, was he that shot at the drum before: Wherein they also entreated to have faire warrs, with promise of the same on their parts.

The code of practice was not necessarily applied in all instances. For example during the siege of Kenilworth Castle in 1266, it is rumoured that the herald (drummer/trumpeter) dispatched to parley with the besieged barons, was returned to the besieging force with both hands severed at the wrist. Another account of drummers being targeted, outlines the sheer guts and courage displayed by one particular French drummer at the siege of Tarifa during the Peninsular war. Leading a forlorn hope (suicide mission) a young drummer marched alongside his captain beating the advance amidst the smoke of cannon and the chatter of musket fire; by the time they reached the breach in the walls of the citadel, only the officer and the drummer were left standing. Even when the officer fell, the young drummer, standing on a pile of rubble a few feet away from the British lines, continued to beat out his rhythm. There was however a black hearted musketeer amongst the British who dispatched the boy "like a song-bird blasted from the bough." Such was the admiration of the British for the drummer's bravery though, the perpetrator of the foul deed never owned up for fear of reprisals from his comrades.

Another duty expected of a drummer is outlined in a publication by Giles Clayton in 1591 stating:

When any souldier is slaine, or otherwise dead, the Company shall bring the dead body to the ground, with the sound of the Drum, and such solemitie as his service meriteth and derserveth, if conveniently you may.

11. Drum and Fife Commands – Posture and Motions

In 1638 at the Merchant Taylors' Hall, London, exercises were performed by "Certain Gentlemen of the Artillery Garden" before an audience of "Nobility, Aldermen and Gentry" and according to G. Goold Walker in his *History of the Honourable Artillery Company 1537 – 1947*:

'The proceedings opened with a display and combat by eighteen Targettiers armed with Morions [crested metal helmet with curved peak front and rear], Swords and targets, who made their encounters and varied their figures all according to the distinct sound of their music, then entered twenty two members disguised as Saracens ... their music was a Turkie drum and a hideous noise making pipe made of a Buffolas horn – Next appeared forty members in the Moderne Armes, namely sixteen Muskettiers in Buffe-Coats and Beaver Morions, sixteen Pikemen, one Phife and two Drummes with officers and sergeants they marched round the hall, the drums beating a lofty English March, after which the drums struck an air. The whole body then performed a multitude of Postures of the Pike and Musket to a Posture Tune played by the Phife. These were followed by a series of complicated evolutions performed to the streyn of the Almain Posture Tune.'

Fortunately, some of the early manuscripts of 1638 give an insight into the type of things played by drummers and fifers on that occasion. It is interesting to note that the

A drummer of the 17th century – Note the dimensions of the drum and weighty sticks, the slashed over-sleeve at the shoulders of his tunic (which possibly developed into wings worn by drummers today) the silk sash – perhaps the fore-runner of the cross belt worn by Drum Majors, also the officers feather on his cap. Clearly dressed up to a standard and not down to a price!

17th century fifer – Note slashed over-sleeve, silk sash and feather in the cap. Note too the length of the fife and the carriage of a sword. He appears to be playing his fife 'back to front' but this may be a mistake by the woodcutter. See the illustration of mounted fifers for a similar oddity.

notation uses the 'minima' almost throughout and although the time signature indicates two two time or alla breve, the bar lines appear to be somewhat incidental to rather than actual; being used as a rough guide to the eye rather than dividing the music up into equal divisions. Note too, that the clef appears to be in the early form of the C clef in the Soprano position, fixing the bottom line as 'C'. Music for the fife in written form had been treated without serious regard for some considerable time and little had changed by the time of these posture and motions manuscripts.

This long standing flippancy regarding the fife and its music is borne out by the writer Jehan Tabouret (pseudonym of Thoinot Arbeau) in his *Orchesographie* of 1588 where he is quoted as saying:

> Those who perform on the fife need simply play according to their own pleasure and it is sufficient so long as he keeps time with the drum.

Francis Markham, author of the *Five Decades of the Epistles of the Warre* in 1622 remarks upon a *Book of Instruction for the Fife* as being: " ... an unnecessary study."

Posture and motions, fife tunes – to which musket drills and firing postures were performed to the signalling beat of the drum and fife.

12. The Old English March – Importance of the Drum

It would appear that there was little in the way of formal notation for signals for battlefield manoeuvres much before the 16th Century. One notable exception is that of 'The Old English March' which dates probably from the revival of the military art of the 15th Century.

Sir John Hawkins wrote of it in his *History of Music* 1776 thus:

> That Old English March of the foot was in high estimation, as well abroad as with us; its characteristic in dignity and gravity, in which respect it differs greatly from the French, which, as it is given in Mersennus, is brisk and alert.

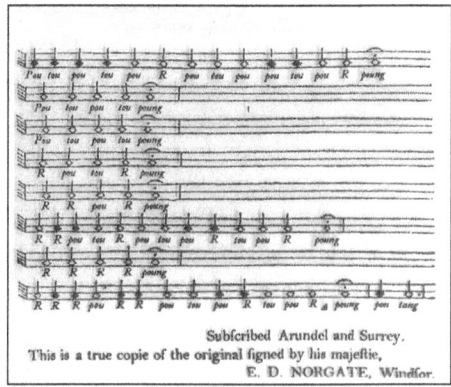

A copy of the Old English March as pricked down by Edward Norgate – *Windsor Herald*.

An amusing anecdote is oft times quoted indicating that Sir Roger Williams, an Elizabethan Soldier, in answering the French Marshall Biron's remark that:

The English March being beaten by the drum was slow, heavy and sluggish.

Replied:

That may be true but, slow as it is, it has traversed your master's country from one end to the other!

With bagpipes and fifes coming into fashion, the exact beating of the English March fell into decline and was all but lost to a generation of drummers. Marshal de Saxe pointed out in his *Reveries* that:

The sound of the drum was something more than a mere noise and that the entire military art depended upon its various cadences.

Francis Markham in his *Five Decades of the Epistles of Warre* related his thoughts on the subject thus:

It is to the voice of the drum that the soldier should wholly attend, and not to the air of a whistle.

So serious was this decline in drumming precision that in 1631/32, a Royal Warrant was drawn up and issued to the City and to the 28 Lords Lieutenant in England and Wales for the better regulation of the Old English March. This read as follows:

Whereas the ancient custome of nations has ever bene to use one certaine and constant forme of march in the warres, whereby to be distinguished one from another. And the March of this our Nation, so famous in all the honourable achievements and glorious warres of this our kingdome in forraigne parts (being by approbation of strangers themselves confest and acknowledged the best of all Marches) was through the negligence and carelessness of drummers, and by long discontinuance so altered and changed from the ancient gravity and majestie thereof, as it was in danger utterly to have been lost and forgotten. It pleased our late deare brother Prince Henry to revive and rectifie the same by ordaining an establishment of one certaine measure, which was beaten in his presence at Greenwich, anno 1610. In confirmation whereof wee are graciously pleased, at the instance and humble sute of our right trusty and right wellbeloved cousin and consellor Edward Viscount Wimbledon, to set down and ordaine this present establishment hereunder expressed. Willing and commanding all drummers within our kingdome of England and principalities of Wales exactly and presicely to observe the same, as well in this our kingdome, as abroad in the service of any forraigne prince or state, without any addition or alteration whatsoever. To the end that so ancient, famous and commendable a custome may be preserved to all posterite.

The manuscript is subscribed:

Arundel and Surrey – this is a true copy of the original signed by His Majesty – Edward Norgate, Windsor.

Issuing the warrant was one thing but teaching the drummers to play the March uniformly was quite something else. In 1634 Thomas Fisher published his *Warlike Directions or The Souldiers Practice*. Fisher, in his preface to the publication offered his credentials as "Having twenty six years experience in the Low Countries and divers years instruction of the trained bands in Kent". He then goes on to give detailed instructions on how the march should be beaten using a series of characters drawn up by him to represent the rhythm and order of beating, quoting:

I have thought meete for the benefit of each drummer which is not yet perfect in the March, to prick down the Old English March newly revived in the plainest form I could invent. Wishing that all drummers would leave off other forms invented either by themselves, or others herein unskilfull, that there may be an uniformity in this Kingdom, as in all other Nations.

His tablature for the various beatings was as follows:
| indicating a strong right stroke
I   indicating a left hand or light stroke
r   indicating 3 or 4 stroke ruff (roll)
2   indicating a half ruff or drag
The end of each phrase being indicated by a full stop.

Thus the Voluntary to the Old English March would be written:
r I | I | r | I | I | | r |.

The selection of these hieroglyphics caused some problems with drummers in deciphering them, added to which was the fact that Fisher was ill served by the quality of his printer's work. How successful he was in his eventual training plan remains a mystery.

Another series of symbols created to aid the teaching of drummers was discovered by Dr Maurice Byrne of the Galpin Society, during his research of the English March, pasted into the end papers of *Hawkin's History of Music* held at the Bodleain Library. These are as follows:

The Grounds of Beating Ye Drum by Francis Douce:

- ⋀ is a stroke and a touch
- / is a plain stroke
- C is four strokes beginning easy and ending hard (I) an half ruffe
- Ɔ is an half ruffe beginning hard and ending hard
- O is an whole ruffe wyth it ye stroke ending hard
- ƆC is a ruffe and a half wyth it ye stroke
- H is a stroke wyth both sticks together
- H' is a stroke wyth both hands and a touch
- ‖ ∕∕ is two strokes wyth one hand and two wyth ye other
- @ is continuall rowling
- L is a bang by ye hoop

Whilst these symbols are slightly easier to comprehend than those of Fisher's, there remains a deficiency in both systems by not establishing a relevant tempo and duration, a deficiency, no doubt, which was overcome by teaching 'parrot fashion'.

In 1635/36 one John Rudd, formerly appointed in 1628 as a drummer in extraordinary and a drummer in ordinary the following year, successfully petitioned the King offering his services in the training of drummers in beating the English March. The year 1636 saw the issue of a directive under signet, to all Lords Lieutenant of England and Wales appointing John Rudd to direct and instruct the drum beaters in all the trained bands:

> ... that there may be a uniformity observed and held constantly in the English March
> and that they assign him and his deputies for this service yearly satisfaction according
> to their discretion.

It is to be assumed that 'the deputies' of Rudd formed a training team, touring the Kingdom and bringing all drum beaters into line with the Royal Warrant – success being rewarded "at their (the Lords Lieutenant) discretion" – a tenuous contractual arrangement at best!

In Maurice Byrne's paper of March 1997, the English March is said to have existed from the early 15th Century until its use was finally discontinued in the early part of the

19th Century. Byrne offers evidence of the existence of no fewer than seven versions of the march using four different notations. Tantalisingly, he also offers versions of the march accompanied by the fife.

Byrne uncovered evidence of the existence of four independent copies of the Charles I document as follows:

- Huntingdon's – From an article in the *Grand Magazine of Magazines* published in 1758, it seems that this copy of the warrant was discovered inside a drum shell and is believed to have been one of those issued to Lords Lieutenant of counties, in this particular case, Henry Hastings, 5th Earl of Huntingdon and Lord Lieutenant of Leicester and Rutland in the 1630s.
- Randle Holmes's – Holmes copied only the preamble and the notation of the Voluntary before the March. The remainder of the march was copied out using only the onomatopoeic words for its beating (eg, Pou, tou, Poung etc). This was cited in the publication *Academy of Armour* Book III, Chapter 9, a publication which was later purchased by the British Museum in 1753.
- Samuel Pepys – In the catalogue of Pepys library compiled by C.S. Knighton in 1981 appears the description of *An Establishment of the Certaine Measure for beating the English March* along with the notation, this particular version being set in two two time.
- Derby's – In 1927, the *Journal of the Society for Army Historical Research* (JSAHR), published a photograph of one of the original copies of the Charles I Warrant, then held at Kneller Hall. The Arms on the Warrant were those of the Stanley Family – Earls of Derby. The warrant was issued to William Stanley, Earl of Derby and his son James, both of whom were Lords Lieutenant of Lancaster and Cheshire from 1626 to 1642. Of the copy once held by Kneller Hall, sadly, there is no trace.

Edward Norgate, appointed Windsor Herald on 28th October 1633, was by trade a lymner (artist of miniature paintings) who was paid £140.00 to produce the *Establishment for the rectifying of the ancient English March* which was signed by the King and distributed throughout the realm as explained earlier.

It must be assumed that the raising of a royal warrant to preserve the English March was somewhat successful given that it remained in use until well into the 18th century and beyond. Its longevity however, was not achieved without change and alteration. Near to its impending demise it had, it seems changed its title from 'The Old English March' to simply 'The Foot March' or even more acute 'March' (8 divisions). In the fife tutors of the day, versions of a fife tune to the English March were to be found in Common time, Half Common time and in Triple time, some tutors even containing three versions in triple time but with variations of notation though still retaining the overall melodic shape.

That the English March was held in high esteem is not in question, since it was beaten on such occasions as state funerals, e.g. the interment in 1695 of Queen Mary I in Westminster Abbey, which bears silent witness: Dirge Anthems for four part choir and organ, oboe band, four slide trumpets, kettle drums and, more significantly, thirty military drummers beating the 'Old English March', all formed part of the funeral procession, thus once again demonstrating the elevated status of drummers and the importance of the drum.

13. Dating the Existence of the Post of Drum Major

It has been suggested that this neglect of the English March by drummers, might have led to the creation of the appointment of the Drum Major in regiments of foot. If this is so then the appointment would only have been established circa 1633/4 following the warrants issue " ... ordaining an establishment of one certaine measure, which was beaten in his (Prince Henry's) presence at Greenwich in 1610..."

The *Dictionary of Musical Terms* (Stainer & Barrett, 1898) indicates that the post of Drum Major was not older than the reign of Charles II since a document dated 1683, makes no mention of the post. There are however, several earlier documents dating from 1632 to 1672 all of which make mention of the Drum Major. Certainly there is evidence of Drummers and a Drum Major belonging to the Coldstream Guards depicted at Monk's funeral in 1670. In *Digge's Arithmetical Warlike Treatise* dated 1579, there is made mention of a 'Chief Drummer'. A later edition of this work dated 1590 has this title amended to read 'Drum Major'.

Clearly drummers had been a part of the royal retinue long before this, especially in military and ceremonial roles. One Janino le Nakerer was listed in 1310 as a King's Minstrel, Edward III had Lambekin the Taberer on his staff. In 1483 Richard III had listed 'taberettes' as did Henry VII, at least one of whom was probably a fifer. It seems feasible then that there must have been someone whose office it was to take charge of these 'minstrels'

In 1552, it is recorded that one Robert Brewer had been appointed as 'Master Drummer of the King's Household' – remaining on the pay lists until 1568. The first known under the title of 'King's Drum Major' (sometimes also called Chief Drummer) was William Gosson, who had been a drummer in ordinary since 1603. He was succeeded on his death, by Robert Tedder in 1629, who held office for but a short time before his death in 1630, which then saw the appointment of William Allen, who retained office until approximately 1646.

1628 sees the mention of a 'Drum Major' who had charge of four drummers and one fifer, a complement which remained on the official establishment of the Royal Household until the 18th Century. Whilst an exact date of the creation of the post is not at all certain, it remains clear from the above that the post is one of long standing and significantly pre-dates the '1633/4' theory, possibly tracing its roots back to the 'Stabstrommler und Stabspfyffer' of the Landsknecht in 1507!

Though the post of Drum Major, in various forms, was evident from at least 1552, as outlined above, the post all but died out during the Cromwellian Period, being seen as 'an unnecessary office', thereafter only first reappearing apparently in regiments of Foot Guards. Official establishment of the post was only made in 1810 but, as stated before, it is considered very unlikely that the Drum Major, in one form or another, did not exist.

The institution of the post of 'Drum Major General' would suggest, by the title 'General', that drum majors were at large in regiments but not exhibiting influence outside of their own regimental boundaries; hence the requirement to recruit, train and licence on a national basis, so that regimental drum majors could continue the training of new drummers once assigned. Similarly, cavalry regiments would almost certainly have had Trumpet Majors, presumably to carry out the same function supported by the authority of the Serjeant Trumpeter, recorded in H.G. Farmer's *The Rise of Military Music* as being one Josiah Broome, appointed as 'Sergeant Trumpeter to the Royal Household' in 1626. He was succeeded in 1641 by Benedict Browne. It is to be assumed that along with the post of 'King's Drum Major', this establishment continued in the Royal entourage until the defeat of the Royalists in 1646, thenceforth becoming another 'unnecessary office'.

14. Cromwell – the Commonwealth and its Influence

During the span of the Civil War in England, the Parliamentarian forces discovered the secret of military success. That secret lay in the creation and maintenance of discipline in the army coupled with financial control. The new national army under Fairfax and Cromwell was born with a silver spoon in its mouth. Parliament could raise taxes to finance its fighting formations and as everyone knows, taxes are limitless! The Royalists on the other hand had to rely on donations from their own well-wishers, even given that some were amongst the wealthiest in the land.

With the issue of an ordnance on 15th February 1645, Parliament demonstrated its financial superiority by authorising and financing the creation of 12 regiments of foot, each comprising 10 companies of 120 men. In addition to the officers, each company was established with two sergeants, three corporals and two drummers. The inclusion of drummers on the company establishment, harking back to the concept embraced by Henry VIII, created a modern precedent which became a tradition; for though the establishment of officers and NCOs varied over the years, the establishment of company drummers remained constant until well into the 20th Century, a span of over 300 years.

In spite of several earlier military mishaps at the hands of the Royalists, Sir Thomas Fairfax and Cromwell now were unstoppable and following the decisive defeat of Charles I Royalist army at Naseby on 14th June 1645, the Parliamentarian 'New Model Army' or 'Roundheads' set about mopping up the remaining Royalist forces, ending with the surrender of the 'Cavaliers' at Oxford in June 1646. Charles I surrendered himself to the Scots who promptly turned him over to the English Parliament. England was now ruled and governed by Parliament, the King remaining a prisoner until his execution in 1649.

Throughout the period of the King's 'imprisonment', the threat of invasion by either the Irish Catholic sympathisers to the crown or by the Scots remained high. Royalist reactionaries in England too raised arms against Parliamentarian forces with the connivance of the incarcerated King. Notably this resulted in the Battle of Preston, where the Royalists were again crushed by Cromwell's force. This was quickly followed by the capitulation of the Royalist garrison besieged in Colchester to a force under the command of Sir Thomas Fairfax. This constituted the era of the Second English Civil War and led ultimately to the King being charged on the 1st of January 1649 as a 'Tyrant and a traitor who had shed the blood of his own people'. By 27th January, the King had been sentenced to death, the warrant bearing sixty-nine signatures of members of the court.

The execution of the King created the conditions for the Third English Civil War – 1649 to 1651. This time the Royalist cause was rooted in Charles II, son of Charles I. The cause was led initially in Ireland by English Royalists and Irish Catholics. In order to deal with the Irish threat, Cromwell took his army to Ireland, where he arrived at Drogheda in September 1649. On 9th September, Cromwell sent his drummers to beat a parley at the town walls in order to petition Sir Arthur Aston, the Governor, urging him to surrender. The text of the petition ran thus:

> Sir,
> Having brought the army belonging to the Parliament of England, before this place to reduce it to obedience, to the end effusion of blood may be prevented. I thought fit

to summon you to deliver the same into my hands to their use. If this be refused you will have no cause to blame me.

I expect your answer and rest.

Your servant,

O. Cromwell.

From Aston, there came no favourable response and so the two forces were resigned to do battle. The defenders of the town of Drogheda numbered but 3,000; Cromwell's army as many as 12,000 – about the right ratio of 'attacker-defender' plus a small reserve force. The battle opened with the English artillery bombarding the steeple of St Mary's Church, Cromwell having been astute enough to recognise its value as an elevated observation post (OP).

The following day the English gunners were directed to concentrate their fire upon the town walls, close to Duleek gate. This battering continued until about 5 pm, when Cromwell issued the order, relayed to the force by his drummers, to storm the broken walls. This action met with strong resistance but, eventually, the Roundheads were inside the town. Once this had happened, according to the rules of engagement of the 17th Century, no quarter would be given to defenders who had refused surrender terms. Aston, along with about 250 defenders, withdrew to the inner fortification of Millmount, an artificial high mound built to the rear of the town, thus severing the chain of command to the remaining defenders. Cromwell ordered all on Millmount to be extricated and put to the sword. Similarly, upon walking up to St Peter's Church, Cromwell was made aware of some 100 defenders who had taken refuge there and in the steeple; Cromwell directed it to be set on fire. Despite the ruthless execution of the military defenders, Cromwell, it seems, was assiduous in ordering that no civilians were to be killed. Shortly after landing in Ireland and before the attack on Drogheda, Cromwell issued the following order:

> I do hereby warn … . all Officers, Soldiers and others under my command not to do any wrong or violence toward Country People or any persons whotsoever, unless they be actually in arms or office with the enemy … …as they shall answer to the contrary at their utmost peril …

This was not necessarily a bout of good will towards the populace but more likely to be a ploy to keep the 'country people' partially on-side for the purposes of obtaining food and water supplies. It is however, extremely unlikely that no 'collateral damage' had occurred during the bombardment and subsequent storming of the town, although with little or nothing in the way of eyewitness accounts of the battle, conjecture and rumour have combined to give Cromwell a bad press.

Cromwell's army then marched south to secure the ports of Wexford, Waterford and Duncannon. Wexford was to be the scene of another brutal battle which historians have listed another atrocity. While negotiations for its surrender were still in progress, Parliamentarian troops, without Cromwell's direction, broke into the town, killing about 3,500 people, of whom 1,500 were simple town folk. Much of the town was raised to the ground. Cromwell's responsibility for the sack of Wexford remains in dispute. Although he did not order the troops to attack, he did little to restrain them or to discover and punish the perpetrators; so much for his fine words pre-Drogheda!

The events at Wexford, coupled with the previous massacre at Drogheda combined to be effective in discouraging some degree of future resistance. The Royalist commander Ormonde stated that the ferocity of Cromwell's army had had a serious effect on his force's morale. As a result, a number of other walled and fortified towns surrendered on terms when bidden. Alternatively, the massacres at Drogheda and Wexford stiffened resolve elsewhere, since some Irish Catholics believed that they would be slaughtered, terms or no terms. Waterford, Duncannon, Limerick and Galway all surrendered but only after having put up very stiff opposition. By now the weather had worsened and the New Model Army was forced to retire to winter quarters where, in miserable and foetid conditions, many of its men, numbered amongst whom would be drummers and trumpeters, died of disease – especially typhoid and dysentery.

The New Model Army met its only serious reverse in Ireland at the siege of Clonmel, where its attacks on the town's walls were repulsed at a heavy cost. The town nevertheless surrendered the following day. Cromwell's behaviour at Clonmel contrasted sharply with his conduct at Drogheda and Wexford. Despite the fact that his troops had suffered heavy casualties attacking the town, Cromwell respected surrender terms that included guaranteeing the lives and property of the townspeople and the evacuation of armed Irish troops who were defending them. The change in attitude on the part of the Parliamentarian commander may have been a recognition that excessive cruelty was prolonging Irish resistance.

There was however, yet much to be done, since the Royalists still held most of Munster. Fortuitously, a mutiny of their own troops in Cork, effectively handed Munster to Cromwell on a plate.

In May 1650, Charles II repudiated his father's (Charles I) alliance with the Irish in preference for an alliance with the Scots. This totally destroyed the morale of the Royalist coalition in Ireland and Cromwell was quick to spot an opportunity to the Parliamentarians advantage. By publishing generous surrender terms for Protestant Royalists in Ireland, many of them either gave up or turned their coats to the Parliamentarian side: All must have felt betrayed by the King and the Royalist cause, especially as the price they had paid had been very high.

Also in May 1650, Cromwell left Ireland to take command of a Parliamentary force, destined to march to Scotland and prevent a Scottish invasion. Henry Ireton, Cromwell's brother in law, assumed command in Ireland with the title and powers of Lord Deputy, with the objective to complete the conquest of the country. Ireton appealed to the English Parliament to publish lenient surrender terms for Irish Catholics, in order to end their resistance, but when this was refused, he began the laborious and bloody process of subduing the remaining Irish by force. The most formidable formation now left to the Irish and Royalists was the 6000-strong Army of Ulster, formerly successfully commanded by Owen Roe O'Neill, whose unfortunate death left an inexperienced Catholic Bishop named Heber MacMahon as the new commander. In June 1650, the Ulster army met a Parliamentarian army at the battle of Scarrifholis, Donegal. The Ulster army was routed and as many as 4000 of its men were killed. In addition, MacMahon and most of the Ulster Army's officers were either killed at the battle or captured and executed after it. This eliminated the last strong field army opposing the Parliamentarians in Ireland and secured for them the northern province of Ulster. For Ireton though there was no glory, he died of disease, in Ireland before the 'final roll of the drums'.

Angry that the English had executed the Stuart king, Charles I in 1649, the Presbyterian Scots decided to invite Charles' son and heir, Charles II, to be the new King. In England, the ruling Council of State saw this act as a severe threat to the security and stability of their fledgling republic. It was therefore decided to send an army to depose the new Scottish king. Cromwell, recently returned from Ireland, was directed by Fairfax to take his army northwards. Accompanying Cromwell on his journey north, was General George Monck, who had a valued reputation as a tried and tested field commander. Monck, Cromwell decided, required a regiment of his own and initially looked to Colonel Bright's Regiment for Monck to Command. However, Bright's Regiment were literally up in arms at the suggestion since they had actually fought against Monck at Nantwich. It was then resolved by Cromwell, on 15th July 1650, to take five companies from Sir Arthur Hazelrig's Regiment and five companies from Colonel George Fenwick's Regiment to form a command for Monk. On 13th August 1650 Parliament placed the new regiment on the establishment, to be known as Monk's Regiment of Foot.

Monk made his headquarters in the border town of Coldstream and the regiment adopted the name as its own, being written up thus:

> The town of Coldstream, because the General did it the honour to make it the place of his residence for some time hath given title to a small company of men whom God hath made instruments of Great Things; and though poor, yet honest as ever corrupt Nature produced into the world, by the no dishonourable name of Coldstreamers.
>
> (Thomas Gumble 1671)

Thus was the regiment formed which later became titled the Coldstream Guards.

Cromwell led his army over the border at Berwick in July 1650. The Scottish general, David Leslie, decided that his best strategy was to avoid a direct conflict with the enemy. Although his army comprised some 22,000 soldiers and so greatly outnumbered the English army of only 16,000 men, most of the Scots soldiers were poorly trained and inexperienced. Leslie chose, therefore, to shelter his troops behind impregnable fortifications around Edinburgh and refused to be drawn out to meet the English in battle. Furthermore, between Edinburgh and the border, Leslie adopted a scorched earth policy thus forcing Cromwell to obtain all of his supplies from England, most arriving by sea through the port at Dunbar.

Whether in a genuine attempt to avoid prolonging the conflict or whether because of the difficult circumstances in which he found himself, Cromwell sought to persuade the Scots to accept the English point of view. Cromwell dispatched his drummers with a message for Leslie, claiming that it was the King that was his enemy rather than the Scottish people, he wrote to his opponents on 3rd August stating:

> I beseech you, in the bowels of Christ, think it possible you may be mistaken.

This plea, however, was unsuccessful.

By early September, the English army, weakened by illness and demoralised by lack of success, began to withdraw towards its supply base at Dunbar. Leslie, believing that the English army was retreating, ordered his army to advance in pursuit of the English. The Scots army reached Dunbar first and Leslie positioned his troops on a hill just south of the town where they overlooked Cromwell's land route back to England. Then, under the mistaken impression that Cromwell was planning to evacuate his army by sea, as indeed, many of his senior commanders were urging, Leslie brought his army down from the hill on which it had been well positioned and approached the town. Witnessing this manoeuvre, Cromwell quickly realised that here was an opportunity for him to turn the tables on the Scots. That night, under cover of darkness, Cromwell secretly redeployed a large number of his troops to a position opposite the Scottish right flank. Just before dawn on 3rd September, following a night of atrocious weather, the English, with drums thundering, launched a surprise attack. The Scottish soldiers in the centre and on the left flank were caught unawares, but managed to rally and hold due to their greater numbers. The right flank however, was being seriously savaged by a superior and experienced Parliamentary force. Inevitably, despite a spirited defence, their lines started to disintegrate. Observing this disaster, the rest of the Scottish army lost heart, broke ranks and fled. In the rout that followed, 3,000 Scots were killed and over 10,000 were taken prisoner, most of whom perished in miserable circumstances on their forced march to the South.

Cromwell had triumphed again and was made firstly the 'Lord General of the Army' and later, under the *Decree by the Instrument of Government dated 16th December 1653*, 'Lord Protector of the Commonwealth'.

> ... the Commonwealth of England, Scotland and Ireland and of the Dominions thereunto belonging, shall be and reside in one person, and the people assembled in Parliament; the style of which person shall be 'The Lord Protector of The Commonwealth'... That Oliver Cromwell, Captain General of the forces of England, Scotland and Ireland, shall be, and is hereby declared to be, Lord Protector ... for his life.

A strict puritan, (who nonetheless drank and smoked and was said to be fond of music) Cromwell presided, successfully but with some ruthlessness, over his rebellious and troubled realm for twelve years. The arrival of this era, known euphemistically as the 'Commonwealth', brought the 'Prison of Puritanism' in which all music, other than psalms or hymns was considered profane.

Ballad singers were arrested and imprisoned, minstrels were suppressed and a high moral and puritanical code was imposed on the land and its wretched populace. The army though was in a quandary, since there remained a need for trumpets, drums and fifes as martial signalling instruments; these being tolerated probably as a necessary evil. The fife though was little used and the position of Drum Major, as mentioned earlier, though not necessarily proscribed, was seen as an "unnecessary office."

Cromwell died on the 3rd September 1658, and barely two years later the Monarchy was fully restored. As an eerie prelude to his ultimate fate, sometime before his death, Cromwell was present before a cheering crowd; he turned to one of his commanders and said humorously;

> The people would be just as noisy if they were going to see me hanged.

This prophetic statement came to a full close on 30th January 1661. By order of Charles II, to avenge the death of his father, Charles I, under the parliamentarian executioner's sword, the exhumed bodies of Cromwell, Ireton and Judge Bradshaw (who had condemned

Charles I to the death penalty) were treated thus:

> This day (to the stupendous and inscrutable judgments of God) were the carcasses of that arch-rebel Cromwell and Bradshaw the judge who condemned his Majestie and Ireton, son in law to the Usurper, dragged out of their superbe tombs (in Westminster among the Kings), to Tyburn and hanged on the gallows there from nine in the morning 'til six at night, and then buried under that fatal and ignominious monument, in a deepe pitt: Thousands of people (who had seen them in all their pride and pompous insults) being spectators, look back ... and be astonished – and fear God and honour the King, but meddle not with those who are given to change.

From the diary of John Evelyn 30th January 1661.

Tyburn gallows stood on the spot where now the junction of Oxford Street, Park Lane and the Edgware Road occurs (Marble Arch), beneath which, somewhere, lie Cromwell's remains.

Part III

The Restoration and Beyond

15. The Serjeant Trumpeter and Drum Major General

The restoration of the Monarchy occurred on the 29th May 1660 at Saint George's Fields, London and with it came calls anew for the re-creation of the musical prowess that had existed prior to the imposition of the Commonwealth, rather in the style of the Germans.

The Germans had formed a special guild, whose purpose it was to recruit, train and licence trumpeters and kettle drummers. These musicians enjoyed special privileges and status, much as their English counterparts had prior to the Commonwealth. The Holy Roman Emperor Ferdinand II granted them a set of imperial privileges in 1632, which were confirmed and revised by subsequent emperors until 1810, when Friedrich Wilhelm III dissolved the guild. Its chief functions had been to maintain the quality of playing and the instrument's status; another was to ensure that pupils, who studied for a period of two years with an acknowledged 'field trumpeter' before his release from apprenticeship, learnt thoroughly the five principal military calls or 'field pieces'. These were 'Boute-selle'(Boots & Saddles), 'A cheval'(To Horse), 'Le Marche'(The March), 'La Retraite'(The Retreat), and 'A l'etendart'(The Attendance).

Whilst music and the fife were now considered acceptable in England, much in the way of expertise had been lost, particularly in the 'training base' – the duties, status and standards of drumming at large were not centrally co-ordinated and it seems that without some form of proper licensing and control the true art of drummers was damned to corruption.

In 1660, one John Mawgridge was appointed into the resurrected post of King's Drum Major, whose job it was to take charge of all the drummers and fifers of the Royal Household. Serving under him were three members of his family. Mawgridge died in 1688 and was succeeded by his son, also called John Mawgridge, who had entered the King's Music in 1671. By 1689 the appointment was merged with that of the office and title of Drum Major General of the Forces, whose job it was to recruit, train and licence drummers for the King's service. Within two years of taking up this dual post, Mawgridge had recruited and trained 144 drummers for his Majesty's Royal Regiments, being paid a fee of six shillings per head. His wages were set at £30 a year, which appears to be about £22 less than the annual cost of his livery, indicating that he was probably a man of independent means.

Detailed research into the post of The Drum Major General has drawn many blanks. It seems likely that the post and its remit might have been copied from the French, given the close relationship betwixt England and France at that time. In 1651, the 'Sun King', Louise XIV, had appointed to his court a 'Tambourin-Major' whose role was similar to that prescribed for the Drum Major General. The returning, formerly exiled, Royalist officers who helped raise the standing army post 1660, would no doubt have been well aware of the French military practice, including 'Le Tambourin-Major'. Whatever the origins, it seems that the post survived for 102 years and was variously held by John Mawgridge, as previously mentioned; John Clothier, who had been Drum Major General of the forces since 1719, and was also "Court-Drummer" (ie, Drum Major to the Royal Household, paid at £24 a year); John Conquest who was recorded as Drum Major General in 1755, and was known to have held that office throughout the period 1762-69 at the rate of £100 a year; Charles Stewart (3rd Guards) of whom little is known, and finally taken over on the 3rd March 1791 by William Hood of the Coldstream Guards. By the mid-1700s though, the post was largely one of grace and favour and not at all useful in the recruiting or training of drummers. The Royal Household though continued to retain drummers, since in 1888, John Day, who had previously been listed among the court musicians as "solo violinist", became "Household Drummer." The diminution in the efficacy of the post of the Drum Major General however, might be explained by the changing face of battlefield command.

16. Last of the 'Sovereign Generals'

On 10th June 1727, George, Elector of Hanover, succeeded his father to the throne of England as King George II and ruled for thirty-three years. Militarily he had gained experience of commanding on the battlefield under the Duke of Marlborough at Oudenarde, and was later to personally command his army culminating in the defeat of the numerically superior French Army at Dettingen in 1743.

Doubtless, he would have had his cavalry signalling by trumpet and his infantry operating to the beat of drum and fife. More significantly though, this was the last occasion when a British sovereign commanded his troops in battle and arguably thereafter as a result, trumpeters, drummers and fifers began to see a decline in their privileged status. The already stated declination of the purpose and terms of reference of the Drum Major General appears to coincide almost exactly with the change of Sovereign Generals. Instead of trumpeters, drummers and fifers being recruited nationally for training and subsequent licensing, it is believed that this was eventually to become a wholly regimental function.

Little is known about the role of the Serjeant Trumpeter but it must be safe to assume that it carried a similar job description to that of the post of Drum Major General. So, the Serjeant Trumpeter recruited and trained trumpeters for the cavalry. What is not clear is whose responsibility it was to recruit and train Kettle Drummers, the Serjeant Trumpeter or Drum Major General? It is suspected to be the former rather than the latter but the demise of the former probably traced the same route as that of the Drum Major General.

As the role of the Drum Major General diminished and with it too the role of Serjeant Trumpeter it is assumed, as previously mentioned, the role of the Drum Majors and Trumpet Majors of regiments increased. Though the post of Drum Major was not to be properly established until 1810, from the foregoing, it is doubted that any regiment existed without the presence of a Drum Major.

With national recruiting of drummers now a thing of the past, the additional burden for recruitment fell upon an already tried and tested source of trainee drummers. All armies in the field required to be sustained; not only in combat supplies such as ammunition, powder, rations et al, but when out of the line, rest and recuperation and other spiritual and physical needs required to be met; these were largely met by the administrative 'tail'. This consisted of the supply train, comprised of the 'quartermaster' (sic) and the official supply network who provided combat support and all military essentials to sustain the 'F echelon'. In addition there would be the unofficial support network such as vendors, cooks, suppliers of ale and liquor, tailors, cobblers, saddlers, leatherworkers and in many cases wives and families (and other 'ladies') of the fighting men, termed the 'camp followers'.

Many of the soldiers had sons who, when of age could be enlisted as 'drummer boys'. The advantage for the regiment was a steady but fairly sure supply of young drummers, with supple wrists and quick minds, for comparatively little outlay. The advantages for the family were increased income from the boy's pay and one less mouth to feed and clothe due to the boy being brought into rations and uniformed as a serving soldier. Additionally it could be argued that the boy now faced a future in an honourable career, provided he survived! Additionally the boy drummer recruited from the camp followers would most probably be capable of speaking one or more foreign languages, if not fluently certainly workable. This element of his 'education' came from prolonged contact with allied troops from other nations during lengthy campaigns; for instance Swiss or German mercenaries, French prisoners of war et al.

It is often thought that boy drummers began to be recruited into English regiments only from about the early 1700s but in fact long before that, boys had formed a significant part of military formations in every army that ever existed. The Greeks, Romans and Celts all trained and used boy soldiers in their formations. In Greece, these apprentice soldiers were taken into military training schools and taught the art of soldiering from a tender age. Greek boy soldiers acted as servants to the Hoplite infantrymen. Others were trained as musicians, doubtless operating as flute players and trumpeters. Sparta, the arch-enemy of Athens was said to train their warriors from 'the cradle to the grave' – new-born males being left out overnight; if they survived the ordeal, they were considered suitable for 'Spartan Life'. The feared and highly efficient Turkish fighting force known as the 'Janissaries' recruited boys from across the Ottoman Empire. Once every few years, they would trawl all countries of the Empire and select the brightest and fittest seven year olds, taking them away to Constantinople to be indoctrinated and trained to become 'boy warriors'.

English regiments were inclusive of boy soldiers also; for instance, the well recruited, fed, clothed and administered 14th Century army of Edward III, considered a model of efficiency in those days, was a case in point. This army consisted mainly of two elements: the 'Men at Arms' and the 'Archers': knights, who travelled mounted, were part of the 'Men at Arms' contingent. Apart from three or four horses to serve him, each knight employed two pages to clean his armour and tend to the horses. Many of these pages were boys. It is important to note that in medieval England there was little distinction between man and boy; if the latter was strong enough to wield a sword or draw a longbow, he would automatically take his place in the ranks of combatants, regardless of age. Others were used in the role of apprentice tailors, saddlers or harness makers – others were trained and used as drummers.

By the mid-1700s the obvious source of enhanced recruitment requirements was now coming more than ever from the multitude of male offspring emanating from the train of 'camp followers' – who were not imbued with special privilege, or status apart from the importance of their signalling role.

Even given the continued emphasis on the recruiting of drummers, from whatever source of supply, the roots of their demise as military signallers were becoming imminent. The noise of battle had been increasing both in quantity and volume, consequently drums and fifes were no longer easily heard. Nor was it always possible to distinguish properly the calls or signals being beaten by the drum. During the War of American Independence, the use of the bugle horn (originally the horn of the bugle ox or wild ox) had been adapted to use as a signalling instrument. Its clear sound in the dense forests carried well and was a good deal more portable and versatile than the cumbersome side drum. It was the beginning of the end for the drum and fife as the predominant signalling instruments, their role now being aligned more with ceremony and marching. Their decline though was gradual. Copies of *Drum and Fife Duty* were being published by the War Office until well into the 19th Century.

For a period of time, starting from about 1677, the fife fell out of fashion, being eclipsed by the new-fangled 'hautbois', the fife continuing in its debased role until its revival in about 1747. During the comparatively short time between the re-introduction of the fife and its ultimate demise, the number of instructional manuals for it rose to a veritable flood. Not only did regular regiments have their corps of drums, so too did many regiments of volunteers, fencibles and militia which developed and died between 1793 and 1815. The sight and sound of a regiment headed by its corps of drums marching along the much-improved roads of the time must have been quite stirring. With the coming of the military band though, mainly comprising paid, civilian musicians, came a greater variety of instrumental sounds. All this, coupled with the greater musical repertoire and better musically educated and trained musicians, caused the drummers and fifers to fall behind in prestige. Consequently the band was more likely, through its duties, to come into contact with the officers and the public. Nevertheless, when hostilities beckoned, it was the drums that were projected to the fore, literally when the 'drums began to roll'. On the march too, it was the drums that held sway since the comparatively small bands had difficulty projecting their 'voice' along the marching column.

17. Post-Napoleon

The end of the Napoleonic Wars at Waterloo in 1815 saw the British army reduced to a peace-time establishment. However, this did not change the manner in which regiments conducted their affairs. There was a demand for training publications for fife and drum; businesses sprang up to meet the demand for instruments and uniforms, the latter being developed in the more glamorous style of peacetime. Red tunics (later scarlet) remained the dress for ceremonial; from 1846 however, khaki uniforms, which had emerged in India were brought into universal use in South Africa (ca. 1890+). With these, Foot Guards drummers wore whitened buff equipment, drum carriages, leg aprons and flute pouches. Regiments of the line might be similarly equipped though more often than not wore the same accoutrements in polished brown leather.

Meanwhile, the telegraph at Blandford Camp was demonstrating improving technology in communications behind the battalion. By 1880, the drummer's signalling role with his drum on operations was to be minimal. The bugle however, continued in use as a signalling instrument right up to World War II. The 1880s also saw the final demise of fifes in Highland regiments, pipers having been properly authorised in 1854. The bugle though, remained. 1872 is the blanket time given for many of the major army reforms instigated by the then War Minister, Lord Cardwell. It is probably from these reforms that the formation of the drummers into a central corps rather than being allocated at two per company was introduced. Drummers had, it is known, been used en masse by regiments prior to this but such formations were on a one-off basis for particular events or parades. The engraving 'The Relief of the Guard at St James' Palace' ca. 1790 demonstrates this and interestingly shows the fifes to the fore of the drums in the manner of pipe bands today.

Cardwell is also credited with the regularisation of regimental marches which have survived, in principle at least, to this day. One oddity of the Cardwell regularisation of marches was that apparently the Foot Guards alone had official slow marches. It is seriously doubted though that any regiment did not have its own slow march.

In spite of all the campaigning throughout the period 1881 to 1914, the growth of the most magnificent full dress uniforms occurred. The period also saw the development of drummers accoutrements such as dress cords, drummers swords, regimental staves (as opposed to the issue items), gold tassels worn on the staff of Foot Guards Drum Majors when in state dress (which continues to this day), the full buff equipment including the striped ticking bag, rolled and strapped to the side drum and even in some regiments, the bass drum too. Whilst many of these items had been in use previously, they continued to develop throughout the period.

In this fashion corps of drums approached the end of the 1800s and into the 1900s equipped very similarly to today but still with a positive role in a large army with Empire-wide tasks; a lot of ground over which to march. It was a time when the drums played for anything at the battalion's whim; for church services, for welcomes, departures, football matches, boxing nights, the Regimental Sergeant Major's birthday et al. Additionally there would have been the traditional tasks such as retreat, tattoo, funerals and parade side drummer. Foot Guards drums performed Guard Mounting in London and Windsor and were required to furnish a drummer for each of the detachments at Buckingham Palace, St James' Palace, The Tower of London, Windsor Castle and the Bank of England Picquet. All these in addition to the Queen's Birthday Parade, State Opening of Parliament, State visits and other Royal, State or National occasions.

Drum and flute duty or the English Duty was not unknown either and this tradition is still called for on a monthly basis in Standing Orders for the Coldstream Guards.

The Great War saw tremendous losses on both sides, amongst them there undoubtedly would have been many drummers. Corps of Drums would not have had much in the way of musical duties to perform whilst in the trenches, their primary role being stretcher-bearer. They might though have been drawn together once back from the front to entertain or to add musical accompaniment to marching troops. By contrast, the bugle was often to feature in trench life both in routine calls and to lift the spirits when going 'over the top'. It seems that this practice differed from one regiment to another and the true extent of its use is not known.

It was not until metalled roads became general that marching in step for any appreciable distance, with or without music, became viable. However, the Great War saw a huge increase in the use of motorised transport for lifting troops speedily from one area to another, creating a fluid and flexible means of troop transport that did not require drummers! Drummers were not entirely discounted in this mechanical revolution however: Brigadier General James Jack was transferred from the Cameronians to command the 2nd West Yorks. One of his first priorities was to re-form the Corps of Drums and to have them performing on the march with the regiment, beating retreat and playing for mess dinner nights, the latter two clearly when 'Out of the line'.

The Corps of Drums came out of the First World War, as did the rest of the army with much recovering and re-learning to achieve. Youth organisations such as the Combined Cadet Force, Army Cadet Force, Boys Brigade et al were producing literally hundreds of fife, drum and bugle bands, the senior members of which might have provided a steady if not copious flow of drummer volunteers for the regular battalions to preserve and augment their corps of drums.

During the period 1918 – 1939, the Corps of Drums recovered to a state probably better than that in which they engaged hostilities in 1914. Many drummers were long service soldiers, some sporting more long service chevrons on their forearm than the drum major's badge of appointment. In general terms men were fitter, better fed, better educated and adept at reading and playing from music. This better state of affairs created wider aspirations and affected all to one extent or another. Garrison life up to 1939 required formal training, drill and barrack administration during the morning and games after lunch. There was time then for individual drummers to fade away to those private spots that musicians tend to find to extend their personal musical skills, even if only to keep the senior drummers from becoming complacent. WWII opened with a typical Corps of Drums comprising of 25 competent drummers. It was to become, of course, a highly mobile war with far fewer formal marches. In consequence the musical role of drummers became much diminished in favour of operating as battalion headquarters defence platoon, with a section deployed to staff the battalion intelligence cell, or as a Bren Gun Carrier Platoon or whatever. It ended with soldiers being co-opted into hastily re-formed Corps of Drums if only in an effort to cope with the rash of victory parades. It was not a simple matter at the time to obtain manuscript paper but in at least one case a Drum Major took pen, ruler and plain paper and created his own. With such invention born of necessity, Drum Major Tom Birkett scored the famous 'Hazelmere' and 'The Adjutant' – marches which are to this day, still the stock in trade for any Corps of Drums. Hazelmere was penned in Palestine in 1947; an original copy of some of the music still exists in the drums library of the 'sleeping' 2nd Battalion Coldstream Guards, now safely held in perpetuity in the keeping of the Regiment's Band Librarian, along with other musical treasures from the pen of Birkett and many others. The end of the war saw Britain continuing to sustain and manage a vast but dwindling Empire. There were, in spite of de-mobilisation, still many regiments making up a large peacetime army, with numerous drummers, many of these being national servicemen. As wartime privations diminished and the country began to get back on its feet, full dress uniforms for Foot Guards and Number 1 Dress (Blues) for Regiments of the Line began to emerge. The first Queen's Birthday Parade in Scarlet was in June 1948, musicians now, though, wearing guardsmens' tunics devoid of wings and gold lacework. This post-war period saw soldiers on peace-keeping duties from India to Hong Kong, to Kenya and Cyprus. It was also the time around the mid 1950s when in-barracks discipline was at its fiercest ever – 'the years of the bull'! The appetite for ceremonial and the nostalgic desire to re-establish the perceived pre-war 'social standards' was almost insatiable. In this atmosphere, drummers were to be in great demand for officers' dinner nights, retreat beatings and sundry other parades or events – musical competence was high. Drummers had time to practice both individually and collectively and it was by no means rare in tented camps to hear flutes and drums cutting through the air playing various slow troops and selections from the London shows such as *White Horse Inn*, *The Arcadians*, *Chu Chin Chow* et al – not to mention various Gilbert and Sullivan renderings. There existed too, a greater sense of tolerance and even enjoyment on the part of other soldiers to hear such musical entertainment, often whilst seated around a communal bonfire with a licence from the commanding officer for the quartermaster to issue bottles of ale for the company or battalion 'smoker'. The simple pleasures of the 1950s gave way to the 1960s where there was to be a complete sea-change.

Following centuries of tradition, the recruitment of boy drummers direct into UK service battalions came to an end circa 1958, when 'Junior Soldier' training companies were formed. Boys could enlist from the age of fifteen (the school leaving age) and train for two and a half years whereupon, at seventeen and a half they were recognised as adult soldiers, placed on 'man's pay rates' and posted out to their designated service battalion. The stated object of, for instance, 'The Junior Guardsmens' Company' – established as part of the Guards Training Battalion at Pirbright Camp in Surrey was:

To train drummers and tailors for the Brigade of Guards.

It was a simple concept which followed almost exactly the earlier traditions of the English (British) regiments by providing a steady stream of 'boy drummers' to the eight battalions of Foot Guards comprising the Brigade at that time. Scots and Irish Guards also received Pipers from the Company. Any boy that proved to be non-musical, was simply switched in trade training from the Drums to the Tailors' Shop. Later developments saw the expansion of trade training to include signallers, motorcycle dispatch riders, pioneers, butchers, cooks and by 1960, junior musicians too. At its peak in the 1980s-90s, the 'company' was around 1200 strong and in addition to the specific trades mentioned above, proved a useful supplier of trained infantry soldiers to the service battalions at home and abroad. In the 1960s, considerable resources were employed to ensure that Junior Guardsmen were educationally qualified with the opportunity to obtain the Army Certificates of Education (ACE) 3rd Class, Second Class (EFP) and up to two out of four subjects towards the ACE First Class (EFP Advanced). Thus a bright student might complete his education in three terms and then transfer the remaining educational time in the training programme to 'trade' training. For drummers and pipers especially, this could mean up to two years dedicated trade training in musical skills. Such a student, under the rules at the time, would have been educationally qualified to gain promotion up to and including substantive, adult WO II. It is believed that the other Divisional Depots conducted boy soldier training in similar fashion to the Guards system, providing a steady flow of high quality, well trained drummers and soldiers to the service battalions.

The end of conscription came in the early 1960s and as a result, came also an increased reliance upon the recruitment of boy soldiers to provide the fount of trainees for almost all drummers to service battalions. The profusion of youngsters available to the army was resultant from the hugely increased birth rate post WWII. Born to parents who were more worldly aware and in many cases more travelled via service life, with a new, free National Health Service and compulsory education up to the age of 15; these young men had greater material and social aspirations than those who had gone before. In 1960 the rate of pay for a junior drummer was £2.5s.6d (227.5p) to which would be added 1/6d (7.5p) clothing allowance per week. If the lad had gained promotion to say, Lance Corporal, a further 1/9d (8.75p) would be added, making a grand total of £2.8s.9d (247.5p) minus 3/5d (approximately 17p) for National Insurance contribution, leaving the princely sum of £2, 5s. 4d. (about 230p) per week. Typically, from this, at pay parade each week, the lad would be paid ten shillings (50 pence), less any stoppages for deficiencies or barrack damages, there might be seven shillings and sixpence (37.5p) left to spend for the week. Any remaining pay being put into 'credits'- in addition his feeding and keep whilst on leave would augment his worth by 6/2d per day (about 36p) so that a boy, going home, might pay adequately for his keep whilst in the bosom of the family.

All junior drummers were encouraged, nay obliged, to open and subscribe to a Post Office Savings Book (the POSB known universally as the 'Posby') this forced savings plan was topped up at the rate of 7/7d (about 37.5) per week from his basic pay, giving a satisfying collected wad to delve into when appropriate.

Junior drummers, once having passed out from recruit training, could 'walk out' of barracks at weekends, wearing plain clothes but only if those plain clothes had been seen and approved by the Platoon Commander, Company Commander or Adjutant. This was effected by the soldier concerned dressing up in his best and being marched in on orders to have his apparel approved for venturing beyond the barrack gate. Once thus approved, the 'rig' would be listed in exact detail on the soldier's 'Permanent Pass' – a small red booklet which had to accompany the soldiers ID card (MOD Form 90) upon 'booking out' at the guardroom. Thus equipped, the sergeant of the barrack guard could exercise his venom by checking the lad's dress against that which was listed on the Permanent Pass. Any discrepancy, different coloured tie, shirt or shoes for example, would almost certainly require the lad to return to his barrack room to find the clothing of conformity before being let out. Failing that, it was off to the NAAFI or for adult soldiers, the beer bar, to recount the tale or to dress into uniform for the night out, provided one again passed muster at the guardroom!

In spite of all the barriers to relaxation and enjoyment, by the early 1960s it was not unusual for drummers to be seen in foreign stations, hiring a car to take a girl to a drive in cinema. The mid-sixties also saw the rise of hippies and a kind of horizontal youth culture by which challenge to and disrespect for established values and expectations had tinged almost all classes. With Kennedy President in America, things young and modern were hugely in fashion. These were hardly the right circumstances for the army's senior music to battle through the difficult decade fast approaching. 1970 saw the arrival of the 'military salary' by which an unmarried drummer would receive nearly twice his previous income. There were other factors to which affected the army's senior music:

- The school leaving age was to be increased from 15 to 16 years in August 1974 and as a result those would be junior drummers, came to their craft at least one year later than previously. In consequence far less time was available to learn their music skills; furthermore, the bountiful supply of school leavers previously enjoyed was to diminish.
- Saturday working had largely ceased and so drummers had more time to spend their money, booking out for the weekend and going home to mum! This broke the routine of weekends spent in barracks, some of which at least might have been spent perfecting personal skills on flute or side drum. The art of a drummer takes much time to acquire: It is lost more swiftly.
- The army's task was primarily in Germany, for which mechanised infantry battalions were equipped with armoured personnel carriers; vehicles whose maintenance took the lion's share of working hours at the expense of drums practice.
- Japanese technology produced transistor radios giving instant music and on tap entertainment. The drummers performing skills being at least slightly less significant. A drummer might have been forgiven for thinking 'why bother'?

- All soldiers had watches so arguably the Guard Drummer was not really necessary and in many regiments was done away with as an antiquated idea. Additionally, in the modern and fully professional army, it was felt that private soldiers should have the task of waking themselves. With the disappearance of such bugle routines as reveille and a formal lights out went also such disciplines as boys standing to their beds at tattoo, hand and foot inspections and post lights out inspections. This was seen to encourage the youth culture's demands to be free from tradition – something perhaps the Corps of Drums world was to come to regret.
- Educational development led many NCOs to have at least the qualifications of their officers which, when coupled with the foregoing comments concerning increased personal responsibility, led to a more egalitarian service.

In short, the result was that there were fewer drummers coming through the system and those that were had rather more time, more freedom and more money with which to enjoy themselves. There was substantially less inspiration and encouragement to work at their music in order to sustain the standards set by their forebears. With regimental bands being greatly in demand in many regiments, the drummers tended to lurch on in the background as best they could, rather like a musical afterthought than in the dashing, bold style previously displayed.

In 1977 a further telling body blow was dealt; the advent of the '650 battalion'! By this, commanding officers were obliged to turn the corps of drums into a full time infantry platoon. Gone at a stroke was 95 per cent of practice time; gone in a decade were many experienced drum NCOs and in consequence, gone was much of the musical expertise for the ensuing generation of Drum Majors. After this, and with no central training organisation, the Corps of Drums of all infantry divisions deserve unstinted congratulations for sustaining this form of military music at their separate divisional depots.

18. TA to the Rescue – The Corps of Drums Society

1977 was the year in which a bunch of Honourable Artillery Company Drummers, fearing the worst for the future of the 'Drums, had the sense to form themselves into the Corps of Drums Society. Given everything above, if the society were to be of value and to be successful, it would be a formation that happened in the nick of time.

The society addressed itself to many things. Those of Army relevance were:

(a) The writing and publication of trade standards
(b) The writing and publication of *The Drummer's Handbook* and its accompanying cassette (Army Code 71333)
(c) Recording and distributing 'Training Videos'
(d) Writing and publishing the *Drum's Instructor's Manual*
(e) Writing and Publishing the *Arranging Pamphlet*
(f) Making all ranks, but especially officers. Aware of 'Drums problems'
(g) Studying the continuation training of drummers, 'drums NCO and Drum Majors and preparing educational systems to meet any defined deficiencies as best the society is able. (The society can, for example, prepare correspondence courses or pamphlets; it cannot establish an Army school)
(h) Helping and advising Quality Assurance Directorate liaison with instrument

manufacturers
(j) Advising battalions on uniform detail

Perhaps as a result of these activities, battalions have, by 2011, taken greater interest in the Corps of Drums, though this has not always been beyond the 'give them a scarlet tunic' mode. Drummers themselves have been active too, so numbers are slightly higher and playing slightly better. Of the playing it has to be said though, that few line 'drums know by heart more then 15-20 tunes, whereas a minimum of 50 is by no means an unreasonable number to which to aspire.

Throughout history drummers have needed encouragement and time in which to perfect their art. This has not changed. Where possible they need to be free of routine guards and fatigues; a freedom which results in a bill to the riflemen who undertake a slightly larger share of the chores and a bill which drummers meet by all the Battalion and garrison events they so richly enhance.

19. The Phoenix Arises – the Rebirth of the Drum Major General

The situation was to remain, largely unchanged until 1993. Under the reforms set in place by the Conservative Government's 'Options For Change', individual drum schools at divisional depots such as The Guards Division at Pirbright, The Queen's Division at Bassingbourne, The Prince of Wales' Division at Lichfield in Staffordshire and The King's Division at Strensall Barracks Yorkshire, were all closed down and merged into the newly established Drums/GPMG (SF) Company, under command of Major M.L.A. Hall Coldstream Guards, a former Drum Major. (Note for civilian readers – The General Purpose Machine Gun (GPMG) could be used in the Light Role, using its integral bi-pod or used in the Sustained Fire (SF) Role, mounted on a tripod).

The parallels betwixt the post and remit of Officer Commanding Drums/GPMG (SF) Company and the post and remit of the Drum Major General of the 1600s outlined above, are plain for all to see – in that it now became the lot of the newly appointed 'Drum Major General' (sic.) to recruit and train drummers for Her Majesty's Regiments of Foot Guards and Infantry of the Line.

Initially the company formed part of the Infantry Training Battalion (ITB) at Helles Barracks, Catterick. The ITB consisted of Guards Training Company, Parachute Regiment Training Company, 'P' Company and Drums/GPMG (SF) Company, inclusive of a Bugle Major and two NCO instructors from the bugles of the Light Division. Also under command but detached in Glencorse, Scotland, was the Highland Piping School, staffed by a Pipe Major and four NCO instructors. By 1993/94, following the final closure of divisional depots and the creation of Army Training Regiments, the ITB ceased to exist and was subsumed into the brand new Phase II Infantry Training Centre, Catterick (ITC (C)) occupying both Helles Barracks and Vimy barracks.

The creation of the Corps of Army Music (CAMus) saw individual regimental bands disestablished and larger more effective divisional bands formed, each now established at Minor Staff Band size of 35; these new bands were also established with the post of Director of Music as well as WOI Bandmaster. More significantly, Corps of Drums once again provided a battalion's first line music and ceremonial with their specialist combat role being that of Machine Gun Platoon. (In mechanised battalions however, the corps of drums reverted to the role of mechanised infantry platoon.)

The training programme for Drums/GPMG (SF) Company at Catterick was of 20 weeks' duration, with up to three such courses running concurrently but on staggered start dates and offering sixty vacancies on each course. These were probably the longest and most intensive training courses for private soldiers ever. Taking into account the requirement for fitness training and progressive load carrying training, a little over 15 weeks of the 20 was available for music skills training.

The final exercise for the GPMG (SF) part of the course was a four day exercise on field firing ranges and dry training areas covering the tactical deployment of gun teams, registration of targets (both silent and by firing) setting up secondary and alternative positions for the guns, reoccupation at night and the live engagement of pre-registered targets. Map Predicted Fire exercises and Target Indication from a displaced OP were also taught and tested. Individual endurance was tested by the need for each man to carry up to 120lbs over 10 miles in 2 hours 30 mins – followed by a tactical deployment of guns and engagement of a live enemy.

The final test for the musical part of the course required the trainees to form a complete Corps of Drums to parade and pass off the square in front of the Commanding Officer. The parade would commence with the drummers formed up in two ranks, in full drill order, carrying instruments, to be inspected by the Commanding Officer, accompanied by the Adjutant and Regimental Sergeant Major. The inspection completed, the drummers would march off the square to 'form-up' in playing order and to march back onto the square to conduct a 30 minute marching display covering slow time, quick time, counter marching, wheeling and static playing which would include Victory Beatings for the side drummers. The Bugles would act as precursor to the parade with a Bugle Fanfare followed by a Bugle March to rejoin the Corps of Drums for a static Fanfare. This would be followed by the Commanding Officer's address and prize giving before marching off the square as a complete formation.

It follows that in order to pass the course, drummers had to be not only bright musically but fit, robust and skilled in the care, carriage, deployment and employment of their machine guns, for which they gained a healthy respect, recognising the tactical importance of the weapon system as a powerful combat multiplier.

Moreover, the drummers themselves earned respect from others, once their regime of training was fully understood. In the early days of GPMG (SF) Company training, the cry from Parachute Training Company was "All drummers are queer" – but as time went on the boys in the Red Berets began to appreciate that the drummers were carrying pretty hefty loads and performing well – the derogatory cries, once familiar as Paras met Drummers on the cross-country routes were replaced by the odd grin and nod of the mutually perspiring fore-heads as the formations passed one another. One incumbent on the GPMG (SF) Course, himself a trained Para, admitted, "It was a good course and the machine gun part was as good a test as anything he'd done previously"!

Formal drummer training remains centralised at the Drums Training Company (now titled the 'Army School of Ceremonial'). The established and formal operational Role of 'Machine Gun Platoon' has been removed; instead Corps of Drums have a slightly different war role being employed mainly as the 'Fire Support Group' in infantry battalions. The overall course consists of eighteen weeks training – Class 3 training taking up six weeks of concentrated music skills interspersed only by physical training. Training for Class 2 drummers will occupy twelve weeks of intensive music and military training in Fire

Support Group tactics. Class 1 courses are of one week's duration and are run at one course per year. Courses for Drum Majors' covering Staff Drill, Parade Cane Drill and related ceremonial drills and procedures all form part of the school's remit.

The school is staffed similarly to the original machine gun company with a commissioned Company Commander and a WOI post as Senior Drum Major Infantry as Company 2ic and technical advisor.

Part IV

Origins and Development of Instruments

20. Origins, Development, Music and the Use of Trumpet and Bugle

It is clear that the very earliest wind instruments, often collectively termed 'shofar', were created from natural sources. Typically they were made from the outer, horny layer of keratin formed on animal horns, especially those of the kudu antelope. Bull or oxen horns were also widely sought, along with smaller and more elaborately curled horns such as those of the goat, mountain goat and the ram. In fact any keratin sleeve found on horns could be utilised. The origins of their introduction remain obscure but even in the earliest accounts of their use they were imbued with a mystique which saw them blown only by a certain class of people, mainly priests. The occasions for using the shofar, in whatever form it took, were predominantly those embracing praise, worship and warfare. Many countries in the Middle East still employ their use in religious ceremonies. Much the same might be said of the sea shell 'horns' used by the South Sea Islanders in their ceremonies and worship.

Unfortunately, apart from the earlier section dealing with Roman brass instruments, little has been recorded regarding the actual dimensions of the various trumpets and horns; however, Mersennus, in his *Fifth Book of Wind Instruments*, states:

> I assume then first of all that only six tones of the trumpet are used in the military art, and consequently that only six characters are required for its tablature.

And goes on further to say:

> Thus the military range of the trumpet contains the great system of the Greeks, and the range of the most excellent voices, as is seen in the table that follows.

The six sounds he cites are those of C, G, C, E, G and C. These sounds accord exactly with those based upon the harmonic series possible on an instrument whose dimensions match that of the bugle, i.e. having a tubular length of four feet to four feet six inches. Thus it seems fairly certain that the Greek trumpet and possibly the Roman 'tuba' or straight trumpet might have been of similar size. Confusingly, he goes on to say that a possible

> ... six or seven others could be added to mark the other higher tones, with which tunes are composed.

Paradoxically however, he does not name them but, if correct, this would indicate either a tube nearer to twice the length of the bugle, or very advanced lip technique.

With the development of metalworking, it seems highly likely that specific dimensions would have been decided upon in order for trumpeters to sound en masse and with concordance of tone. This would be particularly important if the Greeks were to conduct meaningful competitions in trumpet playing at the Games. Trumpets could be designed and created to order rather than waiting for Mother Nature to oblige. Typical manufacturing techniques for trumpets or bugles would be essentially the same, beginning with a sheet of malleable metal such as copper, brass or for special purposes, silver – this would be hammered around a trumpet/bugle shaped 'mandrel' or former, possibly fashioned in hardwood or cast iron, to create the recognisable shape. Once thus formed, the edges would be trimmed, notched and fitted up to be hard soldered together, after which the joint would be dressed down with a metal smith's hammer and polished to remove any remaining minor imperfections. Later developments embraced the introduction of seamless cold drawn tubing in place of rolled and soldered tubing. Other modern techniques involve high precision laser welding. In the case of the trumpet, the bell of the instrument would have been manufactured by spinning sheet metal using a lathe and various spinning tools, parted off, notched and soldered onto the main tube. The next process to evolve would be the creation of curves to shorten the measured length of the instrument to make it a more user-friendly device. Very early attempts at this saw the introduction of curved trumpets carried by the Romans and much later, the zig-zag tubing (à la Norman boisin) to reduce the measured length, but retain its volumetric dimensions, and hence the harmonic series appropriate to the length of the tubing. This developed into more gently curved shapes with bracing stays fitted across the tubing for extra strength. As metal working techniques improved further, methods of bending tubing without flattening the radius evolved. This was largely achieved by packing the tubes with such as bees' wax or silver sand. A solution made up of a mix of soft soap and water was also used – by filling the tubing with the solution and freezing it, the water would turn to ice but the soft soap would prevent large dendritic crystals from forming. Sometimes, even molten lead was used to prevent flattening. The tubing, thus treated, could then be drawn around a curved former to obtain the required shape. The beeswax, sand, soap mix or lead once withdrawn by heating or shaking out, left a clear curved tube. By such methods much tighter curvatures of tubing could be achieved than hitherto. A much speedier and accurate means of producing the curved sections is nowadays conducted by machines, capable of creating hundreds of curved sections from straight tubular blanks. The blanks are curved by shaped dies but initially, have a flattened shape with an indented groove on the inner radius, giving a cross section rather in the shape of a capital 'B'. These are then placed into a high precision air-tight die and a jet of high pressure air is fired in, expanding the semi-finished blank into a perfectly curved tube of circular cross section. The final requirements might be to fit and join up the various curved and straight sections by use of 'spigot and socket' joints or 'sleeve' joints and the whole assembly soldered together. Soldering in place the mouthpipe and reinforcement of the bell would also be carried out, the latter being achieved by the addition of a brass wired reinforcement ring in the style of the modern bugle or post-horn or more frequently by 'upsetting' and 'rolling' a false wired edge around the circumference of the bell. All that remained was the cleaning and polishing operation. This would typically require the entire instrument to be immersed in an acid/salts bath to 'de-oxify' the surface leaving clean, bright but matt finished metal. This would be followed by rinsing in cold water, drying and polishing on a buffing wheel and finishing by hand.

There are many members of the current trumpet family ranging from the B flat bugle trumpet through the E flat cavalry trumpet to the B flat concert instrument. The E flat cavalry trumpet in use today with Cavalry and those Army Corps with Dismounted Cavalry links, such as the Royal Logistic Corps, and the B flat bugle trumpet (increasingly rare nowadays) are probably the nearest modern equivalent to those trumpets of the ancient armies.

In medieval days the bugle (an uncommon Old French word, also 'cor bugler', or 'bugleret') was one of the smaller of the keratine horns, being made from the natural horn of the young bullock (latin *bucculus* – or bugle ox). It was used for hunting, social, religious and military purposes. Under the Norman feudal array, it became a favoured military instrument. Worn at the hip and carried by means of a shoulder sling, it was immediately at hand to sound calls and signals. Definite calls for this instrument used for hunting have been identified in a French work of the 14th century. An English book, George Turberville's *Noble Arte of Venerie and Hunting* (1576) is similarly endowed with hunting calls. The British Museum is said to be in possession of an even earlier manuscript dating back to the 13th century.

Often it is thought that the bugle did not come into British military use until adopted from the German Jäger formations hired in support of the British during the War of American Independence 1776/83. Whilst it is true that the concepts of light troops and bugle horn signals (in place of the drum) were drawn together during that conflict, it is clear that the bugle had been around and in military service for some time before that, since it was known to have been in use by units of the British army. Grose, in his *Military Antiquities 1786-88*, says that in 1761:

> ... there were some troops of light dragoons who used horns like post-boys.

Further to this, John (James?) Hyde, inventor of the slide trumpet, trumpeter at the Opera House and Trumpet Major of The London and Westminster Light Horse Volunteers, was commanded in 1798 by the Duke of York via the War Office, to compile a book of trumpet and bugle-horn signals for use in the army. Some of these calls had been in use for decades and others newly composed. Hyde added his instruction for playing the new slide trumpet and several march arrangements for trumpets, in with the signals. His draft work entitled *The Sounds of Duty and Exercise for the Trumpet and Bugle Horns of His Majesty's Regiments, and Corps of Cavalry* was passed to the War Office for approval. Failing to realise that this was only a draft, and without consultation with Hyde, the War Office rushed the document into print under an authority dated 29th December 1798 issuing it thereafter to regiments. Unfortunately, the draft contained several printer's errors. Hyde was furious but the War office brushed his complaints aside in peremptory fashion. Hyde though was a determined fellow; in 1799 he corrected errors of notation in the original work and produced a publication of his own, entitled *A New and Complete Preceptor for the Trumpet and Bugle Horn*. These were amongst the first books of their kind, although one James Gilbert, in his *Bugle Horn Calls for Riflemen* (1804), claimed that he had been the first to have arranged and published the *Compleat Duty for the Trumpet and Bugle Horn for the Light Horse Regiments and Associations throughout Great Britain* dated 1795. Bugle calls also appeared in Captain T. M. Cooper's *A Practical Guide for the Light Infantry Officer* (1806).

During the Wars of the Austrian Succession from 1742/48, nation states were obliged to maintain large field armies if they were to avoid defeat in the manoeuvre battle. This concept required large and fairly cumbersome formations to deploy onto the battlefield. Whilst manoeuvring these formations, their flanks might be vulnerable, so it became the practice to deploy lightly armed and equipped skirmishers to protect the flanks. This was coupled with a skirmish line of sharpshooters out in front keeping the enemy's heads down, mainly by identifying and picking off the officers by 'sniping'. These large armies required long and cumbersome supply trains in order to sustain them. It soon became obvious to the more inventive commanders that these supply trains, which were forced to travel laboriously over terrain with at best, inadequate roads, would be highly vulnerable to attack by the light troops used in the skirmishing role, thereby rendering a serious body blow to the forward echelons. Such small groups of lightly equipped, fast-moving troops trained in self-sufficiency and living off the land, could play havoc with such supply trains. Often operating during the hours of darkness and behind enemy lines, not generally recognised tactics in those days, against lightly defended targets they could appear, strike and disappear in minutes, leaving carnage in their wake. Against this kind of attack, the rigidly trained, heavily equipped (average 65 lbs or 30kg each) and strictly disciplined regular soldiers had little defence. Hence it became necessary to fight fire with fire and the concept of light troops in their own right was born.

The prerequisites for these troops were fitness, self-sufficiency, quick wits, courage and high levels of weapon handling and field craft skills. For the Europeans, such men were to be found amongst the frontiers of Austria and the hills and forests of France and Germany. The Grenzers of the frontiers and the huntsmen and foresters of France and Germany proved a fruitful source of recruitment for those nations, heralding the birth of Chasseur and Jäger regiments. In Britain, Scottish Highland troops were the natural choice initially. With their natural field craft skills, their flair for the raid, ambush, blazing fire-fight and rapid withdrawal, they proved to be very effective.

During the War of American Independence 1776/83, the British Army was obliged to use and adapt the skills of firstly their Indian allies and latterly those of their opponents, the former colonists. All regular battalions in theatre, selected troops for specialist training in self-sufficiency (battlefield survival), advanced fieldcraft and weapon handling skills. Clothing, equipment and weaponry all had to be modified to suit the new tactics. Highland soldiers wore not kilts but trews, muskets were discarded in favour of the lighter, shorter rifle. Command and control in the forests in such fast-moving and fluid situations, often fought at close-quarters over unmapped and hostile terrain, was imperative. The drum in this regard was clearly a non-starter. Too cumbersome and prone to damp and damage by branches and thorns, it could rapidly become ineffective until repaired. The European troops, drawn from foresters and hunters brought with them the solution to the problem – the hunting horn!

In the course of the chase, huntsmen maintained contact by a range of calls and signals sounded on a series of differing sized horns. All the horns had a conical bore which produced a sound ideal for penetrating the thick, close forests. Eventually the horns became larger and consequently louder and began to adopt a curved shape for ease of carriage close to the body. The cor de chasse, played by the French Chasseurs and the waldhorn of the Jäger Battalions are excellent examples of these horns that are still in use by them today. The British, already in possession of the bugle as previously mentioned, naturally adopted the system used by the Jäger as a viable and useful operational procedure. The half-moon bugle-horn shape adapted and used by the British light formations became the recognised pattern for the bugle horn. This newly formed corps, which we know today as the Light Division, was something of an 'S.A.S. of its day' – the clumsy drum and its inability to penetrate the dense forests of North America was rendered obsolete. British light formations were augmented in the War of American Independence by Rangers from the loyalist colonists and Jäger (light infantry) formations hired from the Germans. Used in this role in both Canada and America, the Scots and English regiments proved to be very effective. Rather short-sightedly though, after these conflicts, light troops were stood down and returned to a more conventional 'heavy' infantry role.

In 1793 however, upon the outbreak of war with the French, light troops were again raised. A 5th battalion of German light troops was formed to augment the existing 60th Royal Americans, a specialist unit of light troops formed following the Seven Years War in America. The 5/60th was commanded by Baron Francis de Rottenburg, an experienced light troops commander. Under his guidance the production of a training manual for light troops was produced in 1798. Two years later, selected Scottish Highland and other British regiments were to take part in the founding of the 'Experimental Corps of Riflemen', under a Colonel Manningham, later to be officially numbered the 95th but unofficially called 'Manningham's Sharpshooters'. To obtain suitable recruits, for the new regiment an Adjutant General's Order was sent to Colonels commanding the fourteen regiments of foot, requiring,

> ... each to draft two sergeants, two corporals and thirty men for rifle training.

The order also stated that

> ... eight drummers will be required to act as bugle horns, and I request you will acquaint me, for the information of His Royal Highness (The Duke of York) whether you have any in the regiment qualified to act as such, or of a capacity to be easily instructed.

Initially, thirteen drummers were drafted to the 95th, this number eventually increasing to eighteen. Interestingly, several of the regiments making up the 95th were Highland regiments who were permitted to form a unique Highland Company.

Based upon previous experience, it was clearly sensible for the bugle to become the only signalling instrument for these formations. The drummers handed in their side drums and buckled down to learning all the necessary calls, which by 1805 totalled fifty-seven in all. Many had been borrowed from the Prussian Army, others were written specifically for the 95th and other light formations and had either gained recognition or had come into common use soon after 1800. The calls, published in *De Rottenburg's Regulations* were borrowed in their entirety and to these were added those calls from Captain T.M. Cooper's *A Practical Guide to the Light Infantry Officer*, published in 1806. These calls covered every contingency with which the new rifle corps might meet, both in and out of conflict. More importantly, light troops of whatever nationality deployed into the skirmish line, be they German, Portuguese, Gaelic-speaking Scot or Hanoverian – could accurately identify and act upon commonly recognised calls and signals.

In 1812 the bugle appeared in a new shape, with a single coil in its tube. Originally the bugle was pitched in C and issued with a crook for adapting to B Flat pitch. There was even a brief flirtation with a combination B Flat Bugle and E Flat Trumpet. Fitted with a rotary valve for switching easily from one to the other, it thus obviated the need for Royal Artillery and Cavalry Trumpeters to carry two instruments. It was under consideration by the War Office for quite some time but for one reason or another it never caught on. Orders of 1835 suggested that the bugle should be built only in B Flat. During the 1800s it was to gradually replace the drum and fife as the principal signalling instrument both in barracks and for field calls. Drum signals however were used in the artillery until 1856, and the fife continued to display a few of the routine calls as late as the 1890s, the last war office issue of *Drum and Fife Duty* was, apparently, published in 1887. The bugle became the recognised signalling instrument for the British Light Infantry and by a war office order of 1814, light infantry and rifle regiments were permitted to bear the design of a bugle-horn as a badge or emblem.

Following the Crimean war, the Commandant of Woolwich Garrison, Sir Wm Fenwick Williams of Kars, ordered that the Royal Artillery drum and fife band be converted to a bugle band. Thus the Fife Major, James Lawson, who was also the Trumpet Major, undertook the task of training twenty-four youthful buglers to become the Royal Artillery Bugle Band. A man of Lawson's calibre however, soon became frustrated by the limited compass of the bugle's harmonic series, in spite of having written several marches with two or three part harmonies. Lawson contacted the London instrument maker, Henry Distin, to supply him with his patented but not marketed 'chromatic piston attachment' for the bugle. This device, which was inserted between the mouthpiece and the instruments mouth pipe, created a compass of notation akin to that of the cornet. An example of the chromatic piston attachment was previously held by the Royal Military School of Music, Kneller Hall, though sadly its existence today cannot be verified by the archivist.

The modern bugle is of brass or copper and is almost entirely used by the armed forces, or bands based upon their military traditions. It differs from the trumpet in having a wide conical tube. As mentioned above, it was originally pitched in C, with an extra B Flat crook. Even as late as 1933 though, the B Flat bugle was not universally employed outside of the military. The *Drum Corps Guide* printed and sold by the Premier Drum Company, lists not only the regulation B Flat bugle but also a bugle pitched in G but fitted with a slide to tune it to F. Purported to be easier to play, it was cited as the ideal instrument for youth drum and bugle bands. Also offered was a tuning crook which could be used to tune the G Bugle to D. The regulation bugle of the British Army is now in B flat concert only and is treated as a transposing instrument. In other words, the music is written in the key of C Major but the bugle, like the cornet or orchestral trumpet, sounds a note one whole tone lower than written. Only five sounds are required (in France only four) for the various calls and signals. These are the intermediate open notes of the tube generally termed the 'harmonic series'. This ranges from C below the treble stave (middle C) to G above the treble stave. For more experienced players, seven sounds however are possible, by the addition of the B flat and C above the high G.

Although no documentary evidence survives, it is just possible that the British infantry call 'Last Post' was composed by (or at least arranged) by Josef Haydn who was in London under the patronage of King George III, at the end of the 18th century, when it was decided to rationalise bugle calls across the whole of the Army and Navy. Haydn could hardly have been unaware of this decision, and might have assumed an active part in the procedure. This hypothesis is supported by the consideration that some of the bugle calls (e.g. 'Reveille', 'First Post', 'Last Post') are musically quite complex, non-repetitive but very well composed;

possibly representing a concatenation of musical phrases taken from a number of different regimental or naval traditions

Up to the close of the 19th century there were two sets of calls in use by the British Army; *The Trumpet and Bugle Sounds for the Mounted Services and Garrison Artillery and Infantry Bugle Sounds* and *The Regulation Bugle Calls as used by the Volunteer Rifle Corps and Light Infantry*. In 1902 all service calls were assimilated into one manual, *Trumpet and Bugle calls for the Army*. This was revised in March 1966 and remains the standard bugle book for the Army today.

21. Bugles and Trumpets at War

The historic bugle, that evokes such memories of gallantry, was said to have been used by trumpeter William Brittain of the 17th Lancers who, on the 25th October 1854 was orderly trumpeter to Lord Cardigan at Balaclava and therefore took part in that famous military fiasco known as the Charge of the Light Brigade. Before writing off the whole action as barmy, it would be well to look at the events leading up to the charge and the aftermath.

The plain at Balaclava consists of the North Valley and South Valley both running west to east with Causeway Heights running more or less parallel to both valleys dividing the two at the centre. Thus each valley was screened from the other; troop movements therefore only being identified by posting look-outs on the ridge of Causeway Heights. To the west end of the valleys were the Sapoune Heights which had visual access to both valleys, in consequence this was the location for Raglan's General Head Quarters.

On 24th October, the commander of the allied Turkish contingent, manning the forward defences of Causeway Heights, consisting of six redoubts, received news from one of his spies that the Russians were massing to attack the British positions with a force of over 25,000 men. The information proved to be very accurate in its estimate, the attacking force being in fact 22,000 infantry, 3,400 cavalry and 78 guns. At first light on the 25th, the first of the enemy troops were seen to be making a general advance, which was signalled correctly by the raising of two flags over redoubt No 1. It would appear that the signal was correctly identified by only one staff officer. The message however, was quickly conveyed to General the Lord Raglan at his headquarters, whose reply was simply to be kept informed of events. The Russians had crossed the Tchernaya River, to the north-east of Balaclava and were intent upon capturing the British base and the sea port. The advance was centred on the high ground of Causeway Heights, the forward northern slopes of which included the six redoubts. These forward positions also had nine naval 12-pounder guns in close support. The Woronzov road running along the ridge of Causeway Heights was the only usable, firm based, road leading to the to the siege works at Sevastopol, and therefore of critical importance as a communication link between the allied dispositions.

The task of the Turkish soldiers had been to build a series of fortified positions or redoubts in order to oversee and protect this road and to form a part of the defences of Balaclava. These fortifications however, were not completed by the time of the attack, nonetheless, the Turks in Redoubt No1, having been bombarded by thirty guns and five infantry battalions, managed to hold their ground until 07.30 thereby holding the Russian advance and gaining precious time. Of the 500 Turks in the garrison almost twenty per cent were killed or wounded. Eventually the Turks withdrew from their positions in some disarray. Redoubts No 2, 3 and 4 were to follow, the Turkish garrisons fleeing, many being cut down by pursuing Cossacks.

As the Russian infantry and guns were forcing the Turks out of the redoubts, a force of Russian cavalry began to ride up the northern slopes of Causeway Heights, seemingly with the intention of advancing across the South Valley to occupy Balaclava. At the same time the British Heavy Brigade, under command of Major General James Scarlett, was deploying into the eastern end of South Valley with Lord Lucan's cavalry division on the right to protect the flank. Raglan and his staff, looking down from their HQ located on the high ground, could see the two cavalry forces converging. Raglan, considering Lucan's position to be too isolated, sent what was known as the first Order of the Day. The delivery of orders at that time was a largely workable plan but was fraught with problems of ambiguity. For example, an order would be issued by the commander which would then be scribbled down by a senior staff officer (in this case Brigadier General Richard Airey) and handed to a junior staff officer to deliver to the formation commander on the ground. Like all orders scribbled down by Airey during the battle it carried the general gist of what the commander wanted but was far from specific. It read:

Cavalry to take ground to left of second line of redoubts occupied by Turks.

Lucan was baffled and somewhat irritated by the meaningless command, since there was only one line of redoubts and in any case the Turks had already fled. Seeking clarification from the aide who had delivered the order, Lucan was told that he must position his division at the west of Causeway Heights where the French artillery could offer covering fire (not at all what had been written). Lucan, aware of his reputation and nick name of 'Lord Look-on' earned from previous campaigns, was understandably annoyed at an order which made him appear again a spectator. Nonetheless, he complied and the cavalry division began retiring in good order to take up their new positions, during which time, there occurred a short lull in the battle. The Russian cavalry was beginning to climb the opposite side of Causeway Heights and it occurred to Raglan that the real Russian intention was to capture Balaclava and his order for Lucan to move position had been wrong. This prompted the second Order of the Day – which read:

Eight squadrons of Heavy Dragoons to be detached towards Balaclava to support the Turks who are wavering.

The Heavy Brigade, at this juncture, remained unaware of the presence of the approaching Russian cavalry, and remained oblivious of their deployment until they came over the crest of Causeway Heights and began their descent into the South Valley. There, in front of them and marching across their axis of advance, was the Heavy Brigade, which consisted of the Inniskilling Dragoon Guards, 4th Dragoons, 7th Royal Dragoons and 5th Dragoons. As the Russian cavalry continued to pour over the ridge, both Lucan and Scarlett realised that the brigade was committed to do battle. Scarlett carried out a quick combat appreciation and decided to take ground to his right to avoid an abandoned encampment to his left, rather than having to fight through amongst ropes, tent poles and the accumulated rubbish of a nearby vineyard but primarily, to present the centre of his Brigade as a more compact striking force for maximum effect. The Russian commander thought likewise and took ground to the left and as a result, the centres of the opposing forces were positioned opposite to one another.

Trumpets sounded in the enemy mass and with a drumming of hooves and on a three squadron frontage, something in excess of 3,000 Russians were on the move. Inexplicably, as they reached the bottom of the slope, trumpets sounded again bringing the Russian formation to a halt before a shallow dry ditch, which posed no obstacle to mounted troops. Why the commander had halted his cavalry is a mystery since he had overwhelming numerical superiority and the advantage of a downhill assault on an enemy who, only 400 yards distant was still calmly sorting out their dressing with the officers backs toward the enemy.

Scarlett, finally satisfied with the deployment of the Brigade, positioned himself at its head along with his Aide and crucially important, his Trumpet Major, Thomas Monks. Scarlett then gave the order to Trumpet Major Monks to sound the Charge; the Heavy Brigade was moving, gaining pace and velocity over the 400 yards separating the two formations. Described as 'big men on big horses' whose principle war role was to use shock tactics, They were now putting into practice that which they had trained for and demonstrated to an adoring public at reviews and field days – but now, for real: this was the point of no return – it was kill or be killed; the anticipation of combat, the rush of adrenalin, stimulated by excitement and with a touch of terror thrown in, made a heady cocktail.

Because of their disadvantage of attacking uphill, the brigade was probably only moving at eight miles per hour when the leading squadrons smashed into the Russian cavalry, who had made the cardinal mistake of engaging the enemy whilst at a standstill. The Heavy Brigade forced its way into the very heart of the Russian formation whose flanks were in danger of folding around the heavies in a fatal 'lovers embrace' threatening to envelope them. Fortuitously, a reserve squadron of Inniskillings, previously deployed on other duties but which, thankfully, had been sent for by Scarlett now entered the fray and at full tilt over good going crashed into the threatening left flank of the Russians on their weaker bridle hand side bowling horse and men alike over sideways to be ridden down or slain by a sabre. On the opposite flank, Lord Lucan had dispatched the 4th Dragoon Guards to the fray and was galloping fast to bring up the Royals who, under their own initiative were galloping hot foot towards the action. The repeated impact and shock tactics on the enemy led to only one outcome; their spirit broken and their willingness to fight gone, the Russians broke and fled the field. It had taken about five frantic minutes for the Heavy Brigade to engage with and defeat an enemy several times their number for the cost of just 78 casualties, many of whom were wounded. The Russian casualties numbered well in excess of 200.

At about the same time as the heavies became aware of the enemy cavalry teeming over the ridge, a force of four Russian cavalry squadrons detached itself from the main body presumably to carry out a probing reconnaissance towards the British right flank. The Russian commanders may have thought that the way across South Valley would unopposed and theirs to exploit but this was certainly not the case.

In order to avoid presenting his troops as a target for the Russian artillery, Major General Sir Colin Campbell, commanding the 93rd Highlanders had ordered his men to lie down on the reverse slope of their position on the right flank. The Russian cavalry, testing the strength of the defences on the British right remained unaware of the presence of the 93rd until at 900 yards the Highlanders stood up and taking their dressing by the centre, prepared to meet the Russian cavalry, said to have numbered about 500 against the 93rd's 400. Campbell had a poor opinion of Russian cavalry and deigned neither to form square nor form fours; instead, he deployed his men in two ranks to maximise the weight of fire over a broader front.

On Sapoune Heights, the headquarters staff including William Russell, a *Times* newspaper war correspondent, looked on in complete silence as the enemy cavalry and the 93rd prepared for battle. The cavalry began its advance towards the 93rd – at the sound of a trumpet, the canter moved up a gear to a gallop, followed by the sounding of the Charge. The 93rd "...that thin red streak tipped with a line of steel" (Later, famously to be named the 'Thin red line' – embodied by the Argyll and Southerland Highlanders, now subsumed into the Royal Scottish Regiment) bolstered by remnants of the Turkish garrisons from the redoubts, stood firm. At about 800 yards, a ragged volley of musket fire from the Turks proved ineffectual and, shaken by their previous encounters that day – the Turks broke and fled the field, many of the Turkish soldiers being belaboured by a Scottish soldier's wife as they fled through the camp of the 93rd. Undeterred by this action the 93rd brought their muskets to the present; at 600 yards the rolling volley of musket fire, delivered at extreme range appeared to have little effect but gave time enough for the Highlanders to reload. Whilst completing the reload drills, supporting fire from Campbell's own battery and the nearby Royal Marine artillery began to take effect on the cavalry. Still the cavalry came on at full tilt. At about 300 yards the 93rd delivered its second volley, the result of which amazed the Highlanders; whilst several horses and men went down, the Russians reigned in and wheeled away to the left and lost the advantage of the momentum of the cavalry charge. Rather, it looked as if the cavalry were aiming to ride around the 93rd right flank and so avoid contact. Campbell quickly deployed his Grenadier Company to the right flank to take the cavalry in the flanks; this they did to good effect, causing the cavalry to turn and flee disappearing over the crest of Causeway Heights. Thus were the Russian cavalry broken and repulsed; first by the heavies and then by the 93rd, with many a trumpeter sounding the days calls and commands.

As previously indicated, the morning of 25th October had heralded an attack by Russian infantry supported by cavalry on the Allied lines resulting in several positions, namely Redoubt 1, 2, 3 and 4, manned by Turkish troops, being over-run by the Russians. The guns therein were captured before the small party of British artillerymen could disable them.

It was now about 10:30am and the actions of the day so far had favoured the allied force. The defeat of the Russian cavalry in two swift engagements had deprived the Russian commander of a valuable, highly mobile force to use as a forward screen and/or flank protection in his bid to advance on Balaclava. The Russian guns, previously deployed in the North Valley in support of the earlier action by Russian infantry against the redoubts, had now been re-deployed to the far end of the valley to cover the battered cavalry squadrons as they re-grouped and took stock of their position. Russian infantry were also present in some force but were showing no signs of continuing their advance. Raglan's intention was to have his infantry (1st and 4th divisions) advancing simultaneously along the floor of the South Valley (1st) and along the crest and southern slope of Causeway Heights (4th) screened by the cavalry division. However due to a laggardly start from the siege lines at Sevastopol by the 4th Division, they were well to the rear of 1st Division and time was ticking away. Meanwhile, Raglan nursed another fear. It had always been considered by British commanders, that the capture of one's artillery was tangible proof of victory to the opposite side. This had been held as a truism by Wellington who, having been the mentor of

Lord Raglan, ensured the concept remained fixed in Raglan's mind albeit that in the mid-19th Century, this idea was at best a little dated. Nonetheless, it remained axiomatic in the mind of Raglan and was a factor which was to be instrumental in shaping the events that were about to unfold, with disastrous results.

Raglan could see Russian gun teams gathering on the skyline and feared that they were about to limber up the captured British guns from the redoubts and tow them away. This prompted the fateful message that initiated the Light Brigade's actions.

The order for action was given by Raglan, the order was then scribbled out in writing by Raglan's Chief of Staff and passed to another junior staff officer who was directed to deliver the order to the commander on the ground. Such orders may or may not have been augmented by concise verbal instructions as necessary, relayed by the messenger who spoke on behalf of the army commander.

The particular message on this day read as follows:

> Lord Raglan wishes the Cavalry to advance rapidly to the front – follow the enemy and try to prevent the enemy carrying away the guns. Troop Royal Horse Artillery may accompany. French cavalry is on your left immediate.

The order was handed to Captain Lewis Nolan to deliver to Lord Lucan. Nolan was said to be a self-opinionated, vain, volatile officer who displayed an open contempt for both Lord Lucan and Lord Cardigan. Lucan having read the order was prompted to ask for clarification. Nolan replied, "Lord Raglan's orders were that the cavalry should attack immediately!" Lucan was still puzzled. "To Attack Sir? Attack what? What guns Sir?" Nolan, with huge arrogance and not a little irresponsibility, waved his arm in the general direction of the far end of the valley with an insolent "There, my Lord, is your enemy! There are your guns!" The scene was set and awaited only the players to step upon the stage.

Lucan, not surprisingly, was horrified at the task required of his division – that is for them to ride to engage Russian guns at the far end of the valley some one and a half miles distant, and to survive the natural killing ground created by the Russian artillery which had batteries covering the valley on the left on Fedioukine Heights, from the right from Causeway Heights and just to put the icing on the cake, from the guns at the far end of North Valley.

Lucan accepted the order without seeking further clarification and decided that the Light Brigade should lead the attack with the heavies bringing up the right rear of the formation. Not unnaturally, when given the tasking, Lord Cardigan felt at pains to point out the obvious dangers inherent in such a ride but nonetheless, accepted the burden with some misgivings. The Order of Battle for the Light Brigade for the attack consisted of the 13th Light Dragoons, 17th Lancers in the first of three waves; The 11th Hussars in the second wave and the 8th Hussars and 4th Light Dragoons making up the third wave; a total of 678 men and horses and a rough haired terrier by the name of Jemmy belonging to the officers of the 8th Hussars and inseparable from his masters.

At about 11:10am, Cardigan took his position at the head of the Brigade and gave the order to advance first at a walk, then a trot building into a canter. All were terrified at the prospect of near certain death but greater was the fear of letting oneself and ones comrades down, underpinned by regimental pride and discipline.

The order to draw swords was met with a ragged cheer from the cavalrymen as they cantered down the valley. But now the Russian guns from literally left right and centre joined the battle. Lucan, seeing the destruction of the mounted formations before him, ordered the Heavies to pull up and withdraw from the charge. The Light Brigade though carried on; at one hundred yards the Russian infantry began firing – at fifty yards the guns, loaded with grapeshot belched smoke and flying iron into the ranks of the first wave; nevertheless, the sheer momentum of the Light Brigade saw elements of the 13th Light Dragoons and 17th Lancers fall on the gunners of the batteries and with a lust for revenge, dispatched almost all of them by lance or sword and riding through the batteries, set about attacking a formation of Russian cavalry who, having been soundly thrashed previously that day had no stomach for a fight, and fled back to the Tchernaya river from whence they had appeared that morning. The 11th Hussars and 4th Light Dragoons galloped into the fray, quickly dispatching the remaining gunners and rode through to assist the first wave in their pursuit of the Russian cavalry.

Now though, having achieved their (mistaken) objective, what were they to do? The remaining troops were rallied and re-grouped ready for their withdrawal in contact. The Russians, attempted a half-hearted counter attack, the result forced the Light Brigade to move diagonally across the valley therefore exposing themselves to gunfire from Causeway Heights, inevitably sustaining further casualties. Once back on friendly soil, the roll call revealed the true cost of the disastrous action. Of the 678 men forming the Light Brigade at the start, only 195 answered up.

With regard to Trumpeter Brittain's involvement, historians are at odds as to whether the 'charge' was ever sounded by Brittain or any other trumpeter on that fateful day, nonetheless during the Charge of the Light Brigade, Brittain was grievously wounded and later died in hospital.

Sergeant James Nunnerly, describing the event, wrote:

> I got the bugle from under Trumpeter Brittain after placing him on the stretcher. The cord was under his back and to remove it would have given him great pain, so one of the men that was present drew his sword and cut the lines that were under his back, from the bugle.

Later, one of Trumpeter Brittain's nurses referred to him as "a most pitiful case who begged that his bugle should not be taken out of his sight".

Trumpeter Brittain's bugle was sold for £1,600 in two minutes at Sotheby's on the 20th April 1964. Bought through the Parker Gallery it was later presented to the 17/21 Lancers.

Sadly, the exploits of the Light Brigade are not unique. In the fog of war, and predating electronic communications, messages scribbled hastily by the commander and sent by messenger (often a young officer on the General's staff) would be thrust into the hands of a hapless officer commanding a company, regiment or a division of cavalry, with little regard for the fact that, what the general can see from his vantage point and what, if anything can be seen by the sub commander waiting in the wings to be called forward might be very different. The messenger, probably having had to brave shot and shell to deliver the message, was not necessarily in a position to answer any poignant questions as to the exact meaning of what might be an ambiguous directive.

Another example of this misunderstanding of delivered messages also concerns a cavalry action. This time in the German army during the Franco-Prussian War; France had declared war on 15th July 1870 upon Prussia and her German allies. Although the battles that ensued though were far from one-sided by 12th August, Napoleon III, now very much feeling his age and suffering ill health, conceded that modern warfare and the technological improvements in weaponry and tactics were a little beyond him, and with his army withdrawing (though not yet beaten), he left the field and instated Marshal Achille Bazaine as commander of the French Army.

By 15th August, Bazaine had managed to conduct a successful withdrawal in contact bringing the German 1st Army to a standstill. However, the 2nd Army had crossed the Moselle and were advancing in a north-westerly direction with the possibility of cutting the French route of withdrawal. At dawn on the morning of the 16th August, the French situation was deteriorating rapidly. The two withdrawal routes were hopelessly clogged with large elements of a retreating army, along with its 5,000 horse drawn wagons and camp followers. Amidst reports of German cavalry having been seen in the vicinity, Bazaine postponed the move until the afternoon to ease the congestion.

At 09:00 though, German artillery opened the day's fighting, which was to prove to be bitter and hard fought. This included several cavalry engagements of charge and counter-charge, and regiments of infantry embroiled in toe-to-toe slugging matches. Eventually, through rates of attrition on both sides, the fighting was left to the duelling between opposing artillery. By about 13:00, the German III Corps had gained the villages of Flavigny and Vionville but at great cost: they had committed all their infantry reserves during the battle and had suffered serious casualties rendering them barely battle-worthy; the troops were short of ammunition and their left flank was still being ripped apart by French artillery. With the possibility of a flank attack and growing signs of the French gathering for a counter-attack, it was clear that unless something were to be done and done quickly, III Corps would be forced to withdraw or stand fast and risk being defeated in detail. The only thing remaining was the cavalry: the only cavalry available at the time was the 12th Cavalry Brigade commanded by Major General Friedrich von Bredow, located just south of Vionville. Aged 56, von Bredow had gained experience commanding a cavalry brigade during the 1866 war with Austria and had earned a reputation for steadiness and careful planning. His brigade consisted of two regiments; the 7th Magdeburg Curassiers and the 16th Lancers. Both regiments were below battle strength, being composed of three squadrons instead of five.

At about 14:00 written orders were delivered by a young staff officer instructing von Bredow to 'break the enemy infantry opposite you'. On looking up at the target area von Bredow noted that the infantry opposite him was formed up in rear of an artillery gun line: "That infantry?" queried von Bredow, pointing to the enemy behind the guns – "The fate of the day hangs upon it" replied the young officer arrogantly and, wheeling his charger about, took off at a smart gallop leaving von Bredow under no illusions regarding the task beset him.

The experience of the 1866 war now manifested itself in von Bredow – he detached a squadron of lancers to protect his vulnerable left flank and then settled down to conduct what now is termed a 'combat appreciation' or 'mission analysis'. In short he read the ground before him to use as many features and as much cover as possible in order to move his troopers to the forming up place (FUP), ready for the assault. The ground to the left of von Bredow's position offered some cover from visibility and from fire; this was to be his choice. By careful movement of his formation he entered the dead ground on his left and moved along the small valley at the head of which there was a dip in the ground offering cover from sight and fire – this was to be his FUP and the position, directly opposite the right flank of the enemy from where he would launch his assault. So far so good but, as in all these scenarios the X Factor rears its ugly head – this was to be in the form of well-intentioned meddling by an un-informed commander of HQ of 6th Cavalry Division who upon seeing von Bredow trotting towards the front line, believed them to be putting their lives at risk. He immediately dispatched a young staff officer to hand von Bredow an order which read 'Even should an occasion for an attack present itself, no attack is to be permitted'.

Von Bredow's reply was just as terse – " I've already had my orders to attack from General von Rheinbaben and I am just on the point of carrying them out"! Von Bredow had reached his FUP and formed his brigade up ready for the assault. On the left, the Curassiers, on the right, the Lancers. The order to 'Advance' was relayed to the brigade by von Bredow's trumpeter, followed shortly by the 'Trot' – the brigade was moving rapidly toward the right flank of the French infantry positions but due to the noise and smoke of the battle being fought to their front, the French were unaware of the impending threat coming rapidly nearer. Through the smoke at last, the French flank positions appeared; at once von Bredow ordered the 'Charge'; the Curassiers, with long straight swords drawn and extended, roared into the French flank, completely over-running a battery of guns. To their right with lances at the 'Engage' position, the lancers fell upon the French like a storm.

The French were taken by complete surprise and with a token of resistance, rapidly broke and ran. The Brigade charged on, cutting down gunners of a second battery and devastating yet another line of infantry. They were making best use of speed, surprise and momentum, three critical criteria of the assault. It could not last however, and the main body of the French were now beginning to bring to bear more concentrated artillery and rifle fire along with rapid fire from the dreaded French Mitrailleuse machine guns, whose devastating fire power when grouped together, the Germans had come to respect. The Brigade had created carnage and inflicted significant casualties on the French flank formations but inevitably the momentum slows and the attackers begin to lose more horses and men; there comes a time when the wise commander breaks off the engagement to avoid annihilation. With the appearance of the French Dragoons and Curassiers on the Brigade's flank, von Bredow ordered the trumpeter, whose trumpet had been struck by a bullet, to sound the 'Withdraw' and the 'Rally'- the trumpet sounded quite stridently and wildly out of tune but to cheers from the remnants of the Brigade, they withdrew from the engagement, retiring to lick their wounds and to carry out a roll call. Of the 500 men of the Brigade led into battle by von Bredow, only 104 Cuirassiers and 90 Lancers remained. Their ultimate objective had however been achieved by removing the threat to III Corps and by reducing quite significantly the number of trained artillerymen, already in perilous short supply in the French formations. Subsequently, this action was to become known as 'Von Bredow's Death Ride'.

As mentioned earlier, bugles were almost certain to have been used in WWI but to what extent is not fully known. One certain case of the sounding of a brass instrument to rally the troops does exist. It concerns one Lieutenant Colonel John Vaughan Campbell, Commanding Officer of the 3rd Battalion Coldstream Guards.

On 15th September 1916, as part of the Big Push Offensive of the Somme, the 3rd Battalion Coldstream Guards were at the village of Ginchy, which, despite the assurances from the military advisors to Field Marshall Haig that 'following the unprecedented seven days and nights of artillery bombardment there would be little resistance from the Germans', several machine gun positions seemed to be unaware that they were supposed to be hors de combat and were giving the Coldstreamers a very hot reception. The first and second assault waves of the Battalion had been severely mauled by the German gunners and had largely been decimated. Colonel Campbell, understanding the importance of taking the battalion's objective to create a stepping stone for the continued advance of the division, rallied his remaining guardsmen by sounding a hunting horn which he always carried. Hearing the sound of the horn and seeing their commanding officer standing in a hail of machine gun fire waving them forward, brought a rousing cheer from the third wave and along with the remnants of the first and second waves, they joined the action and captured the guns, killing or wounding the enemy. For this conspicuous act of valour, Colonel Campbell was awarded the Victoria Cross.

Possibly the last recorded use of the bugle on active service, was during the Korean War at the Battle of The Imjin River; though not in a true signalling sense, but as an act of defiance.

On the night of 22nd April 1951, the 1st Battalion the Gloucestershire Regiment, as a part of 29 Infantry Brigade, had taken up defensive positions near the Imjin River; 'A' Company was on Hill 148 (Castle Hill), 'B' Company on Hill 144, 'D' Company on Hill 182 and 'C' Company held in reserve. The Battalion Headquarters, Mortar Platoon and 4.2 inch mortars of 'C' Troop, 170 Battery RA were located in the village of Solma-Ri. Above and to the rear of Battalion Headquarters was Hill 235, occupied by the Assault Pioneer Platoon and the Medium Machine Gun Platoon. The Battalion Group's strength including attached personnel numbered 773 officers and men.

That night, at 22:30, hordes of Chinese troops attacked, accompanied by their customary din of howls, screams and whistles. Wave after wave of Chinese were repulsed but at some cost. By first light on the 23nd, 'A' company, now reduced to 1 officer and 53 men, was withdrawn to a new position on Hill 235. Likewise, 'D' Company, also severely mauled, took up positions on Hill 235 (Subsequently known as 'Gloster Hill'). During the course of the morning, it was discovered that the Chinese had cut off the supply route in rear of the Glosters and the commanding officer, Lieutenant Colonel James Power Carne, was informed by Brigade Headquarters that if an attempt to re-open this route, scheduled for the next day, the 24th, failed, the Glosters were to hold their ground at all costs.

The commander of the Chinese 63rd Army decided that he would concentrate his efforts on the Glosters' positions. To this end he put forward the 188th and 199th divisions (each of about 9,000 men) to eliminate this stubborn battalion once and for all. By dusk on the 23rd, the Glosters could see the enemy forming up for the attack. Again at 22:30, the Chinese attacked under cover of mortar and machine gun fire. 'B' and 'C' companies combined firepower, coupled with carefully selected artillery and mortar defensive fire tasks, wreaked havoc amongst the attacking force. However, by sheer weight of numbers, they gained ground to the extent that the artillery's 25-pounders were forced to pull their fire back to within 50 yards of the Glosters' forward trenches. The Chinese now held a ridge which connected the two companies and in the early hours of the 24th, used their advantage to launch a rolling, downhill attack on 'C' Company's positions. The two forward platoons ('8 and 9') were completely over-run, but Company HQ and '7' Platoon beat off the second wave and withdrew to positions on Gloster Hill, along with the mortar platoon and Battalion HQ. At about 08:10, the commanding officer gave the order for the now isolated 'B' Company to fight their way out under cover of artillery fire and to rejoin the Battalion on Gloster Hill. By now the Battalion group numbered 400. The men of the Glosters were exhausted from lack of sleep and their fiercely fought defensive battle. Heavily outnumbered and cruelly depleted, their ammunition low and radio batteries fading, they just refused to quit! By dawn on the 25th it had been realised at Brigade Headquarters that no relief was available for the battalion. The Glosters were now being taunted and mocked by the Chinese who, having gained the high ground, were blowing bugles and whistles. The Adjutant, Captain Anthony Farrar-Hockley, suggested that the Glosters might respond in kind. Fortunately Drummer Eagles' had managed to retain his bugle and with this, the Drum Major, Colour Sergeant Philip Buss, disdaining the cover offered by his trench, sent the notes of the Long Reveille and many other calls echoing around the Korean Hills. Seven times more in the next hour the Chinese attacked and seven times more they were repulsed. The commanding officer was given permission to break out as best he could. The Battalion fought a withdrawal in contact, breaking out in company groups. The enemy finally took 'Hill 235' but at tremendous cost to themselves. Amazingly, only 58 Glosters had been killed in the three-day battle but sadly, many were to subsequently die of their wounds or to perish in captivity.

22. Development of the Side Drum

The side drum, introduced into English use after the Crusades, was originally in the form of the tabor. This was a large and cumbersome instrument, slung around the neck by a drum carriage, supported by one hand and beaten with a single stick by the other. Later, the drum carriage was worn diagonally across the body and the tabor beaten with two sticks. The instrument, now termed a 'drum' (thought to be a corruption of the German 'trom' or 'trommel') and being worn at the side of the body, was not unnaturally termed 'the side drum'. Being a loud instrument, the drum was used not only to beat calls for the regulation of military formations; its rhythmic beat was also admirably suited to use in regulating the movement of soldiers when on the march. According to the *Drummer's Handbook*, the marching tempi used were:

- Ordinary Time. 72 – 75 paces to the minute – the standard pace for all drill movements and in the 18th Century, the usual speed on what passed for roads at this period.
- Quick Time. 100 paces to the minute. Used when forming from column of route into line (deploying). Also used by small parties marching on good roads – hence the alternative term 'quick step'.
- Double Time. 120 paces to the minute. Used when a line was required to change direction by forming or wheeling.

These rates of march and drill movements remained largely unchanged for many years.
An Army Order, dated 1st June 1893, signed by Redvers Buller, Adjutant General, does not give the rates of march directly but cites the following:
"The drum will first beat the time in which the men are to march ... In order to ascertain whether the time is beaten correctly, a pendulum or a plummet may be used. When no pendulum is at hand, a plummet can readily be made by suspending a spherical ball of metal by a string, the length of which, measured from the point of suspension to the centre of the

ball, must be as follows for the different degrees of march:

	Inches	Hundredths
Quick	9	80
Double	5	18

Thus arranged, the plummet will swing the exact time required".

Experiments with this plummet concept reveals marching rates of 100 paces to the minute for quick time and 120 for double time. It is interesting to note that there is no mention of 'slow time'.

A later document, issued by the War Office on the 10th August 1914 indicates the following:

Time. – In Slow Time, 75 paces are taken in a minute. In Quick Time, 120 paces, equal to 100 yards in a minute, or three miles 720 yards in an hour are taken. Except during the first weeks of recruit training, recruits, when not in marching order, will take 140 paces per minute in quick time at drill. In double time, 180 paces, equal to 200 yards a minute, are taken.

... Marching in slow time will be practiced only in the early stages of recruit training, and when required for ceremonial purposes.

In his erudite book, *Music of the Scottish Regiments*, Colonel David Murray cites some alternatives to the above rates of march. His research has revealed the following:

The Ordinary Time (Slow Time) was set at 72 paces a minute; this was based on the conclusions of 18th Century military philosophers that battle evolutions gained in effectiveness if performed in time to the heartbeat. This extraordinary reasoning was also extended to musketry exercises and drill movements. However, in consideration of the loads carried by all soldiers in those days, (60 pounds minimum) coupled with poor roads and rough terrain, this seemed to be sensible.

The Quick Step (Quick Time) was set at 108 paces a minute and used as described above for deploying.

The Quickest Step (Double Time) was set at 120 paces a minute and used as explained above for wheeling or forming.

The Oxford Companion to Music cites march times similarly as:
Slow time – 75 paces a minute
Quick Time – 108 paces a minute
No mention is made of Double Time.

Comment: Ordinary Time still survives in the British Army today but is termed 'Slow Time'. Used exclusively for ceremonial purposes, it is now regulated at 65 paces to a minute. It ceased to be taught to recruits in all but the Foot Guards in 1992. Foot and arms drill is now regulated at 48 movements in a minute using the 'Regulation Pause' of 'One – two three – One'. Quick time for the British Army is set at 120 paces a minute. The Foot Guards on ceremonial occasions however, tend to move at nearer 116. The Light Division's version of 'slow time' seems to be set at about 140 paces a minute and their 'quick time' when passing the saluting dais requires them to 'double' past at 180 paces a minute.

The first recorded instance of the drum in English military use is thought to be at the Battle of Hallidon Hill in 1333, where under the command of Archibald, Lord Douglas, Scottish forces marched upon Berwick, which was under continued siege by the forces of the English King, Edward III. After a persistent campaign of harrying the English throughout Northumberland, Lord Douglas and his 14,000 or so men met Edward's three divisions on a small sloping section of ground. The Scots sent their spearmen into battle in a fearsome charge, which was quickly decimated by a 'blizzard' of arrows. Subsequent actions by the Scots ultimately met with a similar fate, the English archers firing continually on the Scots with devastating effect. Reports after the battle cited Scots bodies strewn for five full miles; these included Lord Douglas and several other notable Scottish nobles and gentlemen. It was chronicled, upon the defeat of the Scots:

This was do with merry sowne
With pipes, trompes and tabers thereto
And loud clarionnes thei blew also.

The drum continued to develop but with little regulation as to specification, there were many differences in size and quality. Upon the return to England from France of the 1st Guards in 1662, they were issued with a warrant authorising the painting of their drums in regimental colours and bearing the Royal Arms. The actual size of the drums is uncertain but it is believed that they measured approximately 22 inches deep and 19.5 inches across. The shell and hoops would have been made from ash wood. The heads were of vellum and the instrument was rope tensioned. It is a matter of conjecture whether snares were fitted or not; it does seem likely however since, as recorded elsewhere, the introduction of snared percussion instruments into Britain probably occurred during the Roman invasion. Engravings from General Monck's funeral in 1670 show drummers and their drums in clear detail but no evidence of snares is to be seen. Again, this could be an engraver's oversight or evidence that snares were not in general use at that time, however the latter seems unlikely. The ash wood shell, once curled into shape, would be joined by nailing the overlapping edges together. This area of the join, which was usually to the drummer's right, had by this time begun to assume a most ornate appearance with the nails being used to join the shell being arranged in elaborate patterns. This area became known as the 'Nail Board' and still exists today, in the form of a coloured panel on the left hand side of the drum, the colour being one of the regiment or units regimental colours.

Paintings of the time indicate what appear to be very heavy drum-sticks in use. Additionally, these paintings indicate the absence of drag ropes and a fairly wide deviation in the size of drums in use, there being clearly little in the way of regularisation. By the last quarter of the eighteenth century, the dimension of drums appears to have settled at 18 inches by 18 inches and the depth of the cord hoops down to about two inches. Around the Waterloo period, drums once again were reduced in size being now 16 inches by 16 inches. The Foot Guards however continued to utilise the larger drum. It is also thought that the brass shell might have been introduced along with the smaller 16-inch drum at the same time.

From about 1815 however, Drum Major Samuel Potter of the Coldstream Guards found that the state of side drum manufacture and supply to the army, was so unsatisfactory that he vowed he could do better himself. So he did: in 1815 he created and established the firm of Potter's. There were two quite distinct branches to Potter's, that of Henry Potter in London and George Potter in Aldershot; the latter of these organisations still surviving and trading today and known colloquially as 'Potters of Aldershot'. The Potter drums, fitted now with gut snares, brass shells and drag ropes, were of superior manufacture which regiments could purchase at their own expense. Drag ropes, established probably at the beginning of the 18th century and used to carry the drum over the shoulder when on the march, were now universal in the British Army.

By the outbreak of the Crimean War in 1854, the Foot Guards had firmly settled on a drum of 14 inches by 11.5 inches which had a brass shell, two inch ash, cord hoops, calfskin heads, whitened hemp cordage, eight buff braces or 'tug ears' and six strand gut snares. Apart from minor variations in the 1900s, the Guards continued to use this drum – it then became known as the Guards' Regulation Pattern Drum. This style of rope tensioned drum with vellum heads and gut snares remained in service with the Foot Guards, and Regiments of the Line right up until 1962/63 when rope tensioned drums, with all their problems with damp weather and high maintenance requirements, were replaced by rod tensioned drums with plastic heads and multiple strand wire snares. These drums measured 12 inches in depth of shell and 14 inches across, although with the addition of 2-inch ash hoops, the external depth dimension of 14 inches is achieved. Sadly, many of the fine rope tensioned drums, emblazoned with their proud and colourful regimental devices and battle honour ribbons, became much sought after for conversion into coffee tables to adorn officers' and sergeants' messes and in some cases, private dwellings.

One notable exception was the 1st Battalion Coldstream Guards, having at the time a redoubtable and fiery Drum Sergeant who, by fair means or foul, managed to assemble a full set of 5 rope tensioned side drums and two rope tensioned bass drums, all bearing the Battalion's heraldry. Though seen as a triumph for him, the Coldstream side drummers were not greatly impressed. Considering the immense difference in preparation time for parade between rope and rod, it was of little surprise. By the late 60s or early 70s, the rope drums resided on the shelf in the drum store, gathering dust. That is, until the appointment of the writer as the new Drum Major in 1974. The rope drums once again saw daylight but under certain circumstances. It was decided by the Drum Major that, once the drums had been refurbished by the drummers, on State Occasions, when he was dressed in State Clothing, the Rope Drums would be on parade. The side drummers remained hugely unenthused by the need to re-discover the necessary skill levels required to fettle a rope drum for parade. That is until the morning of the Queen's Birthday Parade in the June of 1974. The massed Bands, Pipes and Corps of Drums were assembling on the square at Chelsea Barracks, The Drum Majors' appeared in their gold State Livery and the side drummers of the 1st Battalion Coldstream Guards, being part of the Resident Battalion at Chelsea and therefore keeping their drums out of sight from the communal changing areas used by the other Guards, made their entrance upon the square. With brass shells glittering, striped ticking drum cases uniformly rolled and strapped and white rope-work standing out against the scarlet, blue and gold heraldry, they looked immaculate. Immediately they were surrounded by drummers from all other Foot Guards regiments and bombarded with questions. The awe and not a little envy of the others firmly established the tradition of 'State Dress and Rope Drums.' The side drummers never complained again – rather the opposite.

Brief mention must also be made of the introduction of bass and tenor drums. The bass drum first appeared as a large version of the side drum, hung from a drum carriage worn around the neck with the vellum heads facing left and right of the drummer. Its introduction into Britain dates probably from the craze for Turkish music, which swept Europe in the 1740s. Appearing firstly in Austria, Hungary, Prussia and France; Britain was to follow in 1786 (or even earlier) courtesy of the Royal Artillery Band. Military bands based on the Turkish model consisted of oboes, fifes, kettle drums, tenor drums, bass drums, cymbals and triangles. This penchant for Turkish music endured for about 40 years. Prior to World War II, the dimensions of bass drums were commonly 30 inches in diameter by 16 inches in depth. Modern bass drums typically will measure 28 inches by 12 inches. The tenor drum traces the same ancestry in Britain as that of the bass drum. Sometimes called 'the long drum' it is variously known as the 'caisse roulante' or 'caisse sourde' ('rolling box' or 'dull drum' – French), 'wirbel trommel' or 'rolltrommel' ('twirling drum' or 'rolling drum' – German). Somewhat larger than the side drum, it is beaten with felt headed drum beaters which give a fairly muffled tone, especially with the absence of snares.

23. Development of the Fife

The origins of the fife (flute) in whatever form it first made its appearance on the world stage, as with the first percussion instruments, are also lost in the mists of time. What is clear following recent discoveries is that the fife is one of the most ancient forms of musical instrument. Bone flutes dating back to 9000 BC have been discovered in China. There are also claims regarding a fragment of a much older Neanderthal flute said to date, it is claimed by some, back to 45,000 BC being discovered in a Neanderthal campsite by Dr Ivan Turk, a Slovenian palaeontologist. The age of this find is disputed by the academic world but there is tantalising evidence, following detailed analysis of the fragment, that it was constructed to sound a diatonic scale. The line-up of the holes indicates most strongly that it is part of a flute. The distance between each individual hole suggests the instrument could play a combination of tones and semi-tones, hence the belief that it was an instrument capable of playing a diatonic scale. The above mentioned cache of flutes discovered in China are all fashioned from hollow bird bones, and have between 5 and 8 holes. Some thirty specimens were unearthed one being 24cm (9 inches) in length. Remarkably, one of the flutes is still playable: its sound might have been that which accompanied Neolithic rituals or perhaps just drifted over the campfire into the night when civilisation was young. Perhaps it was the first music mankind ever made!

Attempting to unravel the true origins of flutes and their development is not easy, since in early accounts and documents, the word 'flute' is used indiscriminately for both transverse flute and recorder style, end blown instruments. The first traceable mention in Europe of a transverse flute comes from Ancient Greece around about the 2nd Century BC. From there it seems to have spread westward to parts of Europe and eastward to India, China and Japan. During this period of expansion fifes, not surprisingly, were not regulated with regard to specification, dimension, bore size or positioning of finger holes.

Virdung, in his *Musica Getutscht* (1511) on musical instruments goes some way towards a detailed description of the cross blown Swiss fife which during the renaissance in military use carried such alternative names as Swerchpfeife, Fistula Militaris or Feldpfeife. In his *Musica Instrumentalis Deudsch* (1592) Martinus Agricola illustrates three flutes and a fife, describing the difference as being simply that the flute has the bore of an arquebus shot whilst the fife has the bore of a pistol shot. This seems to be without regard to the relative length and therefore the relative pitch of the instruments.

By the 16th century, the transverse fife (flute) made of such as boxwood, rosewood or any other close grained hardwood suitable for turning, was commonplace in Europe as was the fitting of brass ferrules top and bottom to protect the fragile ends from damage or splitting if dropped. It was in the 14th century however, that the fife had become firmly established in the Swiss Alps. Eventually, by common usage, fifes began to conform to certain criteria. Woodcuts of flutes and fifes from this part of Europe are numerous in this period and apart from a brief flirtation of popularity in Flanders, is wholly absent in the remainder of Central and Western Europe, including England until the latter part of the 15th century. The first ever mention of cross-blown flutes in England is in 1492 when in the Privy Purse accounts 'Guilliam' is "...paid £3.10s (£3.50) for "flotes with a case" – presumably he was a court minstrel.

In the last decade of the 15th century and first decade of the 16th century, the use of the military fife appears to have spread rapidly. As mentioned previously, in 1507 at the 'Diet of Worms', the fifes and drums, with their Staff fifer and Staff drummer in charge, were regularised at the request of Georg von Frundsberg, the Landsknecht leader. The adoption of the Swiss fife by German and Burgundian mercenaries (Landsknechts or Lansquenets) and the incessant warfare between France, Germany and Spain of the period, introduced the soldiery and their employers to the fife across northern and western Europe. It appears the English were amongst the first to adopt it for military purposes outside its native area of the Alps and upper Rhine valley. This, as previously intimated, was by the instigation of Henry VIII following his experiences at the Battle of the Spurs in 1513.

The fife now conformed to a given specification, having a cylindrical bore one blow hole or embouchure and six finger holes. Renaissance fifes, including English fifes, appear in most woodcuts to be one and a half to twice the length of the current B flat flute – about the length of an F flute but much narrower in bore and wall thickness, resembling a long cane. By the 1600s, the military fife had largely assumed the general length of the current B flat flute with a bore diameter of 12mm and was itself pitched in B flat.

At his death, Henry VIII left a huge collection of musical instruments including 78

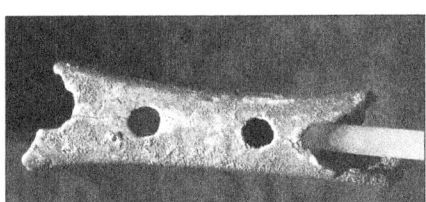

A Bone fragment recovered from an ancient Neanderthal campsite, which is claimed to be the remains of a flute.

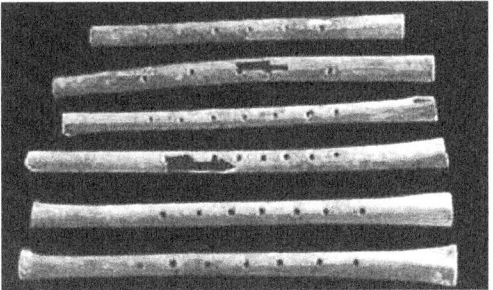

Chinese flutes from 9,000 years BC – note the standard design of six finger holes and one embouchure – the latter being the same size as the finger holes – all made from hollowed out bird bones. (Courtesy of Brookhaven National Laboratory)

From a woodcut showing a rare example of mounted fifers as depicted in the 'Triumph of Maximilian I (1526)' – The Triumph refers to a book of 137 engravings. Note each fifer carries a fife case at his belt to accommodate at least three differently pitched fifes. Paradoxically, one of the three fifers appears to be playing left handed – not impossible, but most unusual.

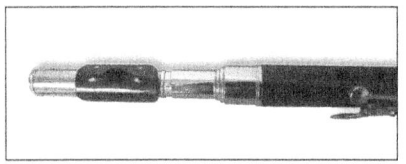

This illustration highlights some of the developments in simple system flute design. Note the metal head joint complete with tuning slide and the cylindrical bore. The creation of the 'chimney' in this case, is achieved by a lip plate.

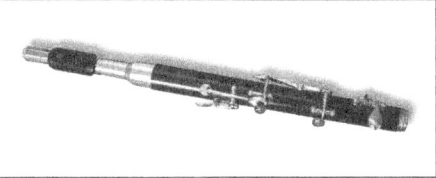

This illustration shows a modern six-key simple system flute, as used by Swiss drum and flute bands to this day. It is a highly versatile instrument pitched in Concert 'C'. With the improved embouchure and the conical bore, it allows for greater power in the lower register with clarity and precision of tone in the upper register.

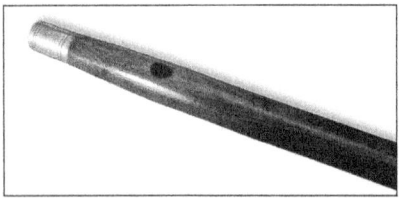

A major development in fife making was the shaping and depth of the embouchure. This change from concentric to ovoid, created greater sonority and power in the lower register.

It may be seen from the illustration of the fife that the external body of the fife widens out to about 22mm in the area of the embouchure. This allows for sufficient wall thickness to create the necessary 'chimney', which forms the correct depth of the embouchure from the exterior to the surface of the inner bore.

flutes and six "phiphes of blacke ebonie" tipped with silver for use as pilgrim staves (walking stick fifes). Fifes were clearly fashionable as well as functional.

Towards the end of the 17th Century however, the fife began to fall into disuse; the last glimpse of it in use is contained in Francis Sandford's *History of the Coronation of James II* (1687), where a fifer, with a bannerol on his instrument, precedes the four drummers of the Royal Household heading the Royal procession.

The cause of the demise of the fife has been apportioned in part to the attitude of regimental officers favouring the bagpipe rather than the fife for accompanying the drum. Whilst the bagpipe remained fairly universal in England until about 1683, it is doubted that this was the real cause even if only because fifers and drummers were on the establishment of all companies – pipers were not! The real cause is more likely to have been the introduction into military music of the 'hautboise' (hautboy) a kind of oboe, taken into use by the Horse Grenadiers in 1678. This new instrument, adopted from the French, who in turn had been influenced by Turkish bands or 'zurnas', was said by Mozart to have "an impudence of tone" which stood out above all other woodwind instruments, even the "squealing of the wry-necked fife" of Shakespeare. From the Horse Grenadiers, the fashion spread into regiments of Dragoons which, being treated as infantry, had side drums. From thence into the Foot Guards and eventually all other regiments of infantry, completely ousting the fife. This 'fifeless' period was to continue for almost half a century. In spite of the French influence in bringing the hautbois into fashion in Britain, they, the Germans and the Swiss retained the fife in its primary role. It is believed that the re-introduction of the fife was again resultant upon outside influences, this time from the Hanoverian and Hessian Mercenaries hired by Britain in its service. The resurgence of interest being led, it is said, by the Foot Guards, Royal Artillery and the Green Howards (19th Foot) whose records show the fife to have been re-introduced into regiments of infantry in 1747.

Following its re-introduction into the army, the fife continued to develop in line with 'civilian' instruments, for which the early 1700s had seen the introduction of the first key, the D sharp key, operated by the little finger of the right hand. This simplified the awkward fingering required for top D and top E, correcting slight imperfections in pitch hitherto found and establishing the way ahead for the transformation from fife to flute.

About 1760 again, following the development of civilian concert instruments, certain London flute makers such as Thomas Cahusac, began to introduce further keywork to military fifes in order to simplify their fingering and improve accuracy of intonation. Clearly, the flute maker had realised that the fife with its given six finger holes (probably best described as 'tone holes') was fairly limited in its choice of key and accuracy of tone. The best keys in which to play the fife are G Major and D Major. The addition of keywork was initially designed to improve tone by allowing additional, and acoustically correctly positioned tone holes to be opened and closed where it would be impossible for the fingers to reach.

These new keys were the Cross F natural key (operated by the third finger – right hand), the G sharp key (little finger left hand) and the B flat key (left thumb), thus creating the four keyed flute. Further additions of the C natural (first finger right hand) and the alternative F natural key (little finger left hand – rarely used) heralded the six-keyed flute in use today. The refinements of separate head joint, metal tuning slide and conical bore for the body of the flute were all in place in concert instruments before 1800, and ergo would have found a ready acceptance in military instruments also. Flutes for Corps of Drums continued to develop, F natural flutes being introduced during the latter part of the 1800s. Certainly, George Potter's catalogue of 1883 features the F natural flute. This was only the beginning, since to follow came the B flat Bass flute, The E flat Bass Flute, The C flat Bass flute, the F natural Bass Flute & finally the E flat piccolo. These all incurred extra expense and apart from the B flat, F natural and piccolo, are rarely seen in service Corps of Drums today.

Flutes/fifes have been made from a variety of materials over the span of their development, mainly constructed from woods such as box-wood (the most prolific), rosewood, cocus-wood, ebony, fruit wood (apple and pear) and African black-wood. Ivory Head-joints were very much in fashion once, as were brass fifes.

By the 1950s and into the 1960s, the design of flutes for military corps of drums saw the following specifications; manufactured predominantly from African Blackwood, furnished with five nickel alloy keys (no alternative F key) – a head joint of cylindrical bore (but no tuning slide), the body section having a conical bore to improve tone and pitching. Tuning continued to be effected by either extending the tenon joint between the head joint and body joint or, more radically, sliding the cork in or out by using a drum stick, more often than not, by a combination of these actions. Tuning (sic.) in those days was, to say the least, a hit or miss affair. These flutes were all constructed in 'High Pitch' and in order to play along with the band in such as Fucik's *Children of the Regiment* or Da Silva's *San Lorenzo*, the head joint for the drummers' flutes had to be drawn out to a little over half the length of the tenon. It was not uncommon then, for a head joint to be seen 'skittling' down the road in front of its hapless owner from time to time.

About 1964/65, following an initiative instigated by the Senior Director of Music, Brigade of Guards, Lieutenant Colonel Rodney Bashford, Grenadier Guards and the Senior Drum Major, Brigade of Guards, Colour Sergeant Peter 'Nippy' Kirk, Coldstream Guards, new flutes were issued to military corps of drums. Constructed from Rose Wood and again furnished with five nickel alloy keys, they were for the first time built in low pitch – that is to concord with Concert pitch of A= 440, (the note of A at 440 vibrations per second – a now universal standard). This, at once, solved the 'skittling' head joint fiasco but being devoid of a tuning slide did little to improve the tuning of individual flutes without recourse to shifting corks. The late 1960s early 1970s saw the introduction of Ebonite flutes; now with six nickel silver keys (alternative F returns) and a metal lined tuning slide. Also built in low pitch, these were of Rolls Royce standard compared to previous issues. These remain, more or less, the standard issue instrument to this day.

Quite often, one hears the argument that high pitched flutes are superior to low pitched flutes, the former being of greater volume. Whilst it remains true that a high pitched sound will carry further than a low pitched sound, the volume output of a corps of drums with moderate skills will be little enhanced by employing high pitched instruments, in the mistaken belief that, by some magical process, their output will be greatly improved. The stark truth is that 'if yer can't play it – it don't make any difference'!

Part V

Dress and Duties

24. Dress

By the Ordnance issued on the 15th of February 1645, Cromwell was empowered to raise 12 regiments for his New Model Army at the taxpayers' expense; drummers continued to be included in the establishment at two per company. These new regiments were, for the first time, uniformly dressed in red.

Previously, regiments had been raised by feudal lords and wealthy landowners who recruited these units from the fit, young and able workers on their estates. Uniforms in very early times consisted of little more than some token or emblem, such as a coloured headband or armband, or perhaps the wearing of a certain flower in the cap. Ultimately, the wealthy landowner aspired to proper uniform dress for his regiment. Since the workers all belonged to him, the feudal lord or landowner saw fit to designate himself as the colonel of the regiment. Each would then decide upon the colour scheme for his regiment, often taken from the colours embodied in his own coat of arms, the result being a kaleidoscope of uniforms in e.g. red, yellow, buff, green or grey. Regiments thus raised were then known as 'Colonel...'s Regiment'. Until quite recently in the infantry of the line only one regiment carried its founder's name, The Green Howards. The Honourable Charles Howard who raised and commanded the regiment from 1738-48, dressed his men in tunics which had green facings on the collars and cuffs. Since there was already another regiment commanded by a Colonel Howard, dressed with buff facings, it became the custom to refer to the regiments as The Green Howards and The Buff Howards. The latter eventually dropping the name of Howard to become known simply as 'The Buffs'! (Later to be titled The Royal East Kent Regiment before subsequent amalgamations sealed its demise).

The earliest document existing relating to the clothing and dress of drummers is that referring to drummers of the Foot Guards, which reads as follows:

"April 1661:- Red coats made up with linings and buttons at the rate of 20/- (£1) a coat. For the embroidering of 24 of the said coats for the drummers at 20/- (£1) a coat. Hats at 5/8d (Approximately 30p)."

Also, on the 2nd June 1661, was issued a warrant to the Master of the Great Wardrobe commanding the painting of twenty-five drums for the Foot Guards in Dunkirk:

CHARLES R
Our will and pleasure is that you forthwith take care for the painting of twenty-five drums for our Regiment of Foot Guards in Dunkirk and for so doing this shall be your warrant given at our Court in Whitehall the second day of June in the thirteenth year of our reign. To our right trusty and right well beloved the Master of our Great Wardrobe for the time being or to his Deputy.
By his Majesty's command
EDWARD NICHOLAS

The design and extent of the embroidery for the coats and the painting of the drums is not listed however, pictorial evidence for the latter, is described further on.

The Royal Regiment of Guards, later Grenadier Guards, drummers of this period wore red coats, lined and faced in blue; Hats were black, in broad brimmed design. It seems that they wore blue breeches, blue worsted stockings with red garters and ribbons. The shoes were black leather with a red bow at the instep.

Drummers of General George Monck's Regiment, The Second Guards (later Coldstream Guards), in 1658 had been similarly attired – black, broad brimmed hat, possibly with feathers at the back; a red coat lined and faced in green, embroidered but without lace-work. Red breeches and stockings completed the outfit. The coat sleeves were buttoned down the seam, evidence of which may be seen on the cuffs of modern tunics today. The lower edge of the coat skirt was cut in a lozenge shaped pattern as were what appeared to be wings at the shoulders. The sash, cuffs and garters would have been green since this was the Lord General's colour; which on the death of Monck in 1670 reverted to blue, the colour worn by other Royal regiments.

The Third Regiment of Guards, later Scots Guards, trace their origins back to 1642. That they had drummers is recorded as a matter of fact but, as to their dress details, little is known. However, according to a Clothing Warrant issued at Whitehall on the 22nd May 1669, the drummers had "read Coates lyned with white."

After the Act of Union was passed on the 16th January 1707, facings of the Scots Guards were made uniform with the other Guards, a change from white to blue. From 1717 the Scots Guards were placed upon the same footing as the other regiments of Guards regarding the supply of state clothing for the Drum Major.

During the reign of George II, the first attempt was made to standardise dress in the Army. An official publication of 1742 entitled *A Representation of the Clothing of His Majesty's Household and all the Forces upon the Establishments of Great Britain and Ireland*, consisted of a series of full colour plates of all regiments of Horse, Foot and Dragoons including a Gentleman Pensioner and a Yeoman Warder. This cumbersomely titled book was colloquially known as *The Cumberland Book* due to the extensive input by the then Duke of Cumberland in its production.

The Royal Warrant issued on 1st July 1751, saw a significant change in drummers dress, when they were ordered to wear complete tunics of the regiments facing colour. These tunics were to be trimmed with regimental lace. Royal Regiments however, were to wear red tunics with blue linings and facings, the coat to be adorned with royal lace. Lacing on the coats of Guards regiments was of blue, edged with orange. The Warrant specifies this as follows:

Drummers Cloathing
The Drummers of all Royal Regiments are allowed to wear the Royal Livery, Vizt. Red, Lined, Faced & Lapelled on the Breast with Blue and Laced with a Royal Lace: The Drummers of all other Regiments are to be Cloathed with the Colour of the Faceing of their Regiments. Lined, Faced and Lapelled on the Breast with Red, and laced in such a manner as the Colonel shall think fit for Distinctions sake, the Lace however being of the colours of that on the Soldiers Coats.

George III, who succeeded his grandfather to the throne in 1760, was no less keen on the subject of details of military dress. He issued another Royal Warrant in 1768; similar in wording to the 1751 warrant, but containing fuller and more thorough regulations for the dress of all ranks.

Drummers and Fifers Coats
The Coats of the Drummers and Fifers of all the Royal Regiments are to be Red, faced and lapelled with Blue, and laced with Royal Lace. The Waistcoats, Breeches and Lining of the Coats to be of the same Colour as that which is ordered for their respective Regiments. The Coats of the Drummers and Fifers of those Regiments that are Faced with Red, are to be white, faced, lapelled and lined with Red; Red Waistcoats, Breeches. Those of all other Regiments, are to be of the Colour of the Faceing of Their Regiments; faced and lapelled with Red. The Waistcoats, breeches and Lining of those which have Buff or White Coats, are to be Red. Those of all others are to be of the same colour as that which is ordered for the Men. To be laced in such a manner as the Colonel shall think fit. The Lace to be of the Colour of that on the Soldiers Coats. The Coats to have no Hanging sleeves behind.

Drummers' coats of the three regiments of Foot Guards were adorned with an extra quantity of lace, referred to in the Clothing Warrants as 'Royal Lace'. This Royal Lace was markedly different in all three regiments. The 1st Guards had white lace with a red strip down the centre, either side of which were embroidered fleur-de-lys; the 2nd Guards had a double row of fleur-de-lys on a plain white ground; the 3rd Guards had dark blue edges, a white strip down the centre and yellow fleur-de-lys embroidered into the blue edges.

Drummers' coats, over the ensuing sixty years from 1768, saw many changes in style and colour. In 1830, drummers' coats for infantry regiments of the line reverted back to red. The single-breasted tunic made its appearance in 1857 and with minor alterations, has remained to this day.

All drummers by now wore a 'mitre' style headdress similar to that worn by grenadier companies. This style of headdress for grenadier companies is said to have been taken into use circa 1677 in place of the black felt tricorn hat. This innovation allowed the grenadier to sling his firelock in preparation to throwing his grenade, without constantly knocking his hat off. For drummers, the cap was embroidered with the regimental device and a drum on the front, with another drum embroidered on the rear turn up flap. There were two, significant factors in this order of dress; firstly, the drummer was immediately recognisable as such by wearing a coat of reversed colours to that of the fighting soldiers, who continued to wear red coats with regimental facings; secondly, the wearing of a drum as a badge on their head dress also served to identify the drummer. Under the influence of George I, the addition of the Hanoverian White Horse on Grenadier style caps was made, along with the motto, '*Nec Aspera Terrent*' (nor do dangers affright us).

The grenadier mitre style of cap was to develop further where, under the 1768 warrant, the specification reads:

Drummers and Fifers Caps
The Drummers and Fifers to have Black Bearskin Caps. On the Front, the King's Crest, of silver-plated metal, on a Black Ground, with the Trophies of Colours and Drums. The Number of the Regiment on the Back Part, as also the Badge, if entitled

to any, as ordered by the Grenadiers.

On the front and rear then, of this mitre-shaped bearskin cap, the drummer would display the drum as outlined previously.

A General Order of 1800 introduced the first shako cap as the regulation head-dress for the Infantry. This ugly, heavy hat was cylindrical in shape and made of black, lacquered leather, the only ornamentation being a large brass plate and a small bristle plume. This was followed by the 'Wellington Shako'- introduced between 1806 and 1811. Made of black felt, it was lighter and smarter than the previous hat, until it rained – whereupon it tended to collapse and somewhat resemble a Breton onion seller's beret fitted with a peak, hardly the dress for asserting moral ascendancy over the enemy. Fortunately, this was replaced in 1815 by the 'Regency Shako' – a much smarter and durable cap, embellished with a large plume, brass plate and chain and laced around top and bottom, it remained in service for twenty-seven years. The only changes occurring in 1835 when it was made of black beaver instead of felt, the plume became a ball tuft and the lace replaced by black leather. In 1844, a new cap was introduced, with small peaks front and rear. 1855 to 1878 saw the last of the shako designs before being replaced by the blue, spiked helmet in service today.

For the Foot Guards, head-dress was eventually to give way to the full bearskin cap, similar to today's bearskin, but now worn by the entire regiment. The distinction of wearing the full bearskin was awarded to the First Guards, post-Waterloo, in recognition of their having faced and defeated Napoleon's elite Imperial Guard, whose head-dress was the full bearskin cap. The Second Guards adopted the full bearskin in 1831, the Third Guards following in 1832.

The 1768 Warrant also saw the introduction of the Drummer's Short Sword – to be worn by all drummers and fifers. This sword was about 20 inches long with a curved, sabre style blade and a curved brass hand-guard similar to that of an officer's sword. The drummer was still considered largely as a non-combatant and the short sword was issued as a part of his dress rather than for fighting.

The dress of Foot Guards drummers, pictured in a series of coloured lithographs of the mid to late 1800s, show continued use of many of the dress details as laid down by The Royal Warrant of 1768. In these pictures the drummer of the First Guards is wearing a white plume on the top left hand side of the bearskin cap, which also bears a large white metal plate to the front, extending down to the bottom of the cap with *Nec Aspera Terrent* plainly visible. As an emblem, the white plume was said to represent the smoke of a grenade fuse and was a recognised distinction of the grenadier companies. Drum hoops are red and bear a curious diagonal blue and white bar design around them. The forefront of the drum shell is decorated with the Royal Arms with lion and unicorn supports, all on a dark blue ground. The drum carriage is plain white with brass fittings and the edges of the buff braces on the drum ropes are red. The coat has the buttons spaced singly.

The drummer of the Second Guards depicted, shows him to be wearing the same style of bearskin cap with a smaller triangular white metal plate, with fur below it, bearing white cord looping and white tassels. He too, wears a white plume (later to become white and red and then finally red – it is not clear why these changes occurred.) The coat, with the exception of the lace as described elsewhere, is the same as that of the First Guards drummers', but with the buttons arranged in pairs. The drum carriage however, is decorated with fleur-de-lys. A peculiarity with the Coldstream drums was the design of the hoops.

These are shown with a blue worm-like line, running around the circumference, painted on a white ground and with red edges top and bottom; a regimental distinction continued to this day. The buff braces on the drum ropes are also edged red.

The drummer of the Third Guards is similarly dressed to his contemporaries but with buttons arranged in threes and a red plume on the top left of the bearskin (latterly no plume at all) with white tassels but no cap lines. A cap plate is worn; smaller than the First Guards but larger than the Second Guards and extends to the bottom of the cap. Drums were adorned with plain red drum hoops. The white drum carriage is decorated with fleur-de-lys. The heraldry on his drum is the Royal Arms and supports; buff braces are pure white.

Tunics for all three Foot Guards show wings to be worn. It is not clear when wings were introduced into the British Army, or for what reason. As mentioned above, evidence of 'what appear to be wings' is indicated in the description of the Coldstream drummer's dress of 1658. A later illustration of a mounted drummer of the 11th Dragoons circa 1742 pictured in W.Y Carmen's *British Military Uniforms* confirms the wearing of wings. Also, Hogarth's painting 'March of the Guards to Finchley' circa 1745, clearly shows wings to be worn.

It is possible that the wing is simply the remaining element of the slashed 'over sleeve' and was used to cover and finish the joint of the armhole seam once the slashed, over sleeve had become just a fashionable band of cloth

The origins of the adoption of the fleur-de-lys are also fairly obscure, some schools of thought being the adoption of the emblem of Old France was brought about by Charles II after his exile in that country. If that is true why was it not incorporated into Foot Guards' dress until 1768? Other schools of thought favour the concept of the French emblem being worn by the drummers to demonstrate contempt for the French Army; this has no basis in fact. Another idea seems to centre on the Foot Guards being sent to France to fight in support of Louis XIV and subsequently being afforded the privilege of wearing the fleur-de-lys in recognition of their services to the French Monarch.

Throughout the Crimean War, the only weapon carried by drummers continued to be the drummer's short sword. The sword now had a straight double edged-blade which was not sharpened, as if to reinforce the non-combatant stance. Later edicts sanctioned the sword should be sharpened but only on one edge. The Mark I sword had an ornate brass hilt with a moulded hand guard set perpendicular to the blade to form a cross. The Mark II sword, issued circa 1895, was three inches shorter at about eighteen inches, with a plain brass hilt and cross style hand guard. In 1903, the Mark II sword, was taken out of service and was not replaced. Buglers wore similar swords but with a cast iron hilt.

With the abolition of the flank companies in 1862, the specialist functions which they had carried out, became embodied in the training and deployment of the rifle companies; drummers, considered now as enlisted men, (or boys) for the first time, were subject to formal military training. This at once created the 'double hatting' continued to this day and designated the ancient art of 'drumming'- with all the accrued privileges and importance once enjoyed, as simply a soldier's job!

1866 heralded the introduction of Crown Lace, known universally as 'Crown and Inch' (or Crown Braid) due to the red crown embroidered, curiously at 'one and three sixteenths of an inch' intervals on the white lace. This replaced the regimental lace previously worn and is worn to this day by drummers of all infantry regiments. Foot Guards drummers continue to wear white lacing bearing blue fleur-de-lys.

Attempting to be definitive regarding the design of lace worn on drummers coats is fraught with difficulties since, a collection of lace held by the National Army Museum Uniforms Collection at the Royal Military Academy Sandhurst, boasts no fewer than 200 different designs.

The issue of Full Dress to infantry of the line ceased with the outbreak of war in 1939 and no other full dress has been issued since then. However, infantry regiments are quite prepared to buy full dress at their own expense in order for their drummers to be resplendent in representing the battalion. It seems logical then for full dress purchased now, to conform to the last official pattern. Excluding the Foot Guards, the official pattern for drummers falls into two categories:

'County' Regiments of the Line; the dress was as follows:

(a) The drummer's tunic was of scarlet cloth with the collar, shoulder straps and cuffs in the facing colour. It was decorated with Crown Lace: two sizes were used. The first being white, three-quarters of an inch wide with scarlet crowns at one and three sixteenths intervals was worn around the front and top of the collar, down the front and back seams of the sleeves and down each back seam with in between, a central line of lace. A further line immediately behind each shoulder strap joined the shoulder seam with the base of the collar. At the waist, a diamond of lace was worn on each of the three back lines, with a button on each of the outer two diamonds. The other type of lace, a quarter of an inch wide with saltire shaped scarlet design at five eighths intervals, was worn around the top of the cuffs, on the edges of the shoulder straps and around the base of the collar. Badges of rank and good conduct chevrons were of plain white worsted material on a scarlet backing. The arm drum badge was embroidered onto a scarlet backing with the shell in yellow, hoops in blue and batter head in white. Wings worn on the shoulder were scarlet, decorated with crown lace and edged with a red and white fringe.

(b) The correct pattern of trousers was dark blue serge with a narrow red stripe along the length of the outside seam of each leg, as worn by the Foot Guards today.

(c) The universal blue cloth helmet, Other Ranks pattern, being of cork was covered with blue cloth and joined with four seams, two on each side; peaks front and back, stiffened and covered with cloth. The edges of the peaks and edge rim of the helmet were bound with black patent leather. There were two ventilation holes situated on each side and on top of the helmet was a brass cross piece, into which was screwed a two and three quarter inch brass spike. The front helmet plate was of brass, in the form of an eight pointed star surmounted by the Sovereign's crown. A regimental device was mounted in the centre of a garter bearing the regimental title. Brass, rose patterned finials were used to secure the brass linked 'curb chain' to the helmet. The curb chain was worn on the chin when on parade but could be hooked up to the rear of the crosspiece when off parade.

(d) The head-dress of the Fusilier Regiments was of black seal skin or racoon. A grenade cap badge to the front and a horse-hair plume on the right, were also worn. A brass linked curb chain was worn on the chin but was never hooked up. Apart from the head-dress, the remainder of their dress was as for the 'County' Regiments.

One final order of dress deserves mention; namely the State Dress as worn by Foot Guards Drum Majors and the mounted bands of the Household Cavalry. The State Dress is the oldest ceremonial uniform in use today, and has its origins in the 17th Century. Upon the death of Cromwell in 1658 the way was clear for the restoration of the monarchy, which occurred in 1660. In 1661 The New Model Army of Cromwell's design was in the process of being disbanded, the last regiment to be scheduled for disbandment being Monck's Regiment – colloquially known as the 'Coldstreamers' due to their service in the border town of Coldstream. In this unsettled time of Charles' reign, serious rioting broke out in London and, the only formed and disciplined body available to the authorities was the Coldstreamers. They quickly put the riots down with great speed and efficiency, much to the delight of the King. The Regiment, by royal invitation formed up on Tower Hill in the presence of the King and laid down their arms to signify no ill will to the monarch and immediately recovered their arms in the service of the king – as a result they were designated by the sovereign the 'Second Regiment of Guards' and along with the First Guards became a part of the Royal Household troops. As a direct perquisite of this the Sergeant Drummer of each Guards Regiment became authorised, by issue of a warrant under Royal Arms to wear the King's Livery in the place and quality of a Drummer to the Royal Household, a tradition that began c.1661 and continues to this day.

By 1678 the musicians of the Life Guards, in recognition of their regiment's loyalty to the exiled king, were dressed in velvet coats laced with silver – the costs being defrayed by the king. In 1707 following the Act of Union, the Third (Scots) Guards having joined the king's service were in 1771 brought into line with the Grenadier and Coldstream Guards with regard to the issue and wearing of State Dress.

The raising of two further regiments of Guards, namely the Irish Guards, formed in April 1900, and the Welsh Guards, formed in February 1915, subsequently saw their Drum Majors dressed in State Dress in line with the other three regiments of Guards

State Dress for Drum Majors, like many other forms of military uniform, has evolved from the original. Examples of such are the wearing of white spatterdashes instead of full length tweed trousers. This requires the wearing of 'item CY – 3395 – Trousers, Short, Drum Major'. These are effectively dark blue knee length breeches which button at the knee and are worn inside the top of the white spatterdashes, which are held in place by a strap buttoned to the waist of the blue trousers. Other examples of this evolution are the blue jockey style hat, the gold fringed red damask silk sash, held in place by a regimental broach and the gold embroidered garters. The colour of the basic coat now being maroon velvet heavily laced with gold and bearing the Royal Cypher embroidered on the chest and back also in gold wire rather than the original silver and of course for Drum Majors the gold tassels worn on the ferrule of the staff. It is generally held that at least some if not all of these innovations may be laid at the door of Queen Victoria and Prince Albert, in their manner of thinking that decisions such as 'lance corporals in the Foot Guards are to wear two white worcested chevrons instead of one since the wearing of one chevron failed to represent sufficient visual authority to the non-commissioned officer posting relief sentries at Buckingham Palace (the latter being purely anecdotal).

25. Drummers and Military Discipline

No history of drumming would ever be complete without some reference to the important but fairly distasteful duties expected of drummers in the field of military punishment, more specifically, the administering of floggings and drummings out.

From the early eighteenth century, corporal punishment consisted largely of whipping, either with a single willow switch or by several bound together to form a 'birch'. This was usually followed by a punishment called 'running the gauntlet' or 'gantelope'. As late as 1777, a publication entitled *Cautions and Advices to Officers of the Army, particularly Subalterns* confirms the practice, with the description of the 'gauntlet' reading as follows:

> There is a punishment called 'running the gauntlet'; in which, if the criminal has a good share of heels, and a little cunning, he may not feel twenty lashes from the whole battalion. It is thus performed: The battalion, under arms is drawn out six deep: the front, third and fifth ranks are ordered to face to the right about, by which three double lines of men, facing each other, are formed. The drummers then give each man a willow switch; and the criminal, naked to the waist, is told to make the best of his way through the ranks from the right of the battalion; he then goes from the right to the left between the first; from the left to the right between the second; and from the right to the left between the third double ranks. Now it is very obvious, from this disposition of the men, that only the second, third and sixth ranks can give the stroke forward, so as to be felt: If the criminal, therefore, has a good share of heels, and runs close to these ranks, he baulks their strokes, so as scarcely to let one in ten of them touch him: and he need not fear the other ranks: for as theirs must be given with the back stroke, he is past them almost before they can put themselves into a proper position.

Later still, in the eighteenth century, whipping or scourging was replaced by flogging, a far more brutal and severe form of punishment. In this the 'Cat-o'-nine-tails' was employed in place of the birch. Initially, the punishment could be inflicted by soldiers or drummers as dictated by court-martial. Eventually however, it became the sole province of the drummer. Sentences ranged from 25 lashes to 1,200. Very occasionally this maximum was imposed but the average sentence called for 300 to 700 lashes.

The ritual was conducted as follows: The Regiment would be drawn up in a hollow square, in the centre of which was assembled a whipping post. The offender, under escort, was marched into the square where his offence and subsequent punishment would be read to all assembled.

Under the supervision of the Drum Major, the offender would be securely lashed to the whipping post and the drummers would be marched onto parade. The lashes would be administered by the drummers, to the steady, rhythmic beat of the drum, each drummer giving only 25 lashes before handing over the cat to the next drummer. The Drum Major would ensure that the drummers 'laid on at a will' or face a taste of the cat themselves. In addition to the Drum Major, on parade would also be the Adjutant, to confirm that punishment had been properly carried out and the Surgeon, to see that the offender did not receive more lashes than he could bear without endangering his life. From an untitled publication of circa 1811, the special responsibilities of a Drum Major regarding floggings concerned the specification of the cat thus:

> It is the duty of the Regimental Drum Major to see that the Cat-o'-nine-tails are properly prepared. He ought also to be particularly careful that no extra ordinary ingenuity is

exercised to make the knots heavier or more searching than the human frame can bear. God forbid that a prevalent report should be true, relative to the insertion of lead in some cats that were used during the Irish effervescence! Left handed drummers ought also to be excused from being the means of adding unnecessary torture, by cutting the back of the soldier across the former stripes, which must be the case when right handed and left handed drummers inflict the lashes.

It was sometimes the case that drummer boys were chosen to inflict the flogging, with the clear intention of increasing the ignominy of the punishment. This was especially so when the flogging was a precursor to the infamy of being 'drummed out'. Generally speaking the drumming out ceremony occurred thus: the battalion would be drawn up, with or without arms, and would line both sides of the route leading to the barrack gate. The prisoner, under armed escort, would be marched from the jail, and brought to the right of the battalion. His offences and sentence would be read out by the Provost Sergeant, often there would also be a parchment pinned to his back describing his misdemeanours. A halter would be placed around the prisoner's neck and the youngest drummer boy would be instructed to take hold of the rope attached to the halter and to lead the man, like a dog, between the ranks; this all to be done in slow-time to the mocking sound of the drums and fifes playing 'The Rogues March' whilst suffering the jeers and spittle of his former comrades in arms.

From time to time the procession would halt and the prisoner's offence and sentence would be read anew, so that all assembled were aware of the gravity of the crime. Doubtlessly this was also to warn off any potential miscreants among the ranks. At each new reading, portions of the buttons and badges would be ripped, unceremoniously from the man's uniform: Finally the entourage would arrive at the barrack gate where, as a final act of degradation, the man was forced to endure a smart kick in the pants by the boy drummer, to send him on his way. Thus dismissed, with only the halter and ruined uniform as his perquisite to connect him with the regiment he had so disgraced.

Grove's Dictionary of Music and Musicians carries a short history of the Rogue's March. The original march was apparently written in two-four time though latterly it is played in six-eight time. Either way, its light hearted and cheerful melody can only have increased the mockery and shame of a soldier thus treated.

As an anecdote, the Rogue's March earned another title. This came to pass during the prolonged campaigns in the Low Countries under Marlborough, where bouts of brief military activity were interspersed with long spells of waiting. Soldiery, when left to such idleness, turns its collective mind to the pursuit of other things. As mentioned elsewhere in this history, the 'Camp Followers' offered recreation of an alcoholic and bodily kind, the consequence of this being an ever increasing number of soldiers being placed 'hors de combat' by sexually transmitted diseases. Marlborough was enraged by this, claiming that he was losing more soldiers to the camp followers than to the enemy. In despair, he ordered the women to be summarily rounded up, like cattle, and to be herded out of the camps without delay. This was duly done and the 'whores' under armed escort and to the tune of the Rogue's March, were drummed out of the military environs. Hence, with typically raucous humour, the Rogue's March was swiftly renamed 'The Whore's March'.

Some two hundred and fifty years later, this historic anecdote was still to the fore, at least in the mind of one drum major (whose identity and regiment will remain esoteric!)

Having promised his drummers a long weekend, away from the dreaded metal monsters that dominated life in Germany, the Drum Major was summoned by the Regimental Sergeant Major, who informed him that the Corps of Drums would be required to play for the Mess Dinner Night on Saturday. In spite of all his impassioned pleas, the Drum Major was outgunned and was obliged to traipse angrily back to the drum's block to break the news. The drummers, many of whom had tickets for 'Blighty' were, to say the least, a tad miffed! So, instead of Saturday being a day of relaxing with a few bevvies, much of it was spent polishing boots, brasses, helmet plates and brushing down their blue cloth helmets.

Come the eve of the dinner and the Corps of Drums, resplendent in their scarlet and blue, formed up in the Sergeants' Mess Dining Room. Given the first nod by the Mess Steward, they came to the ready position; upon the second nod, the drummers launched into playing the Rogue's March (alias 'Whore's March') to play the RSMs wife and all other Mess wives, in to the 'Ladies' Dinner Night'.

It is not on record as to whether the drummers were in on the act but, the gusto with which they acquitted their musical duties, might suggest so. After dinner and further musical offerings from the drummers, the RSM publicly thanked them on behalf of all present and asked "what was the bright little tune by which the ladies had been played in to dinner?" The drum major, without hesitation, replied "It's a traditional tune reserved for such occasions as this, Sir"! Fortunately, the RSM and his assembled dinner guests were woefully ignorant of the history and traditions of the Corps of Drums. Small as it was, the victory of the drummers that night in exacting their revenge for a ruined weekend, was keenly enjoyed.

By orders published on 9th November 1858, floggings and their like were much diminished in the army. Furthermore, in times of peace, floggings were abolished by an amendment to a clause in the Mutiny Bill of April 1868. The last known case of a flogging being inflicted is said to be circa 1880; final abolition coming by way of the Army Discipline Act of 1881. This Act was amongst the many reforms introduced in the army, under the guidance of Lord Edward Cardwell, Secretary of State from 1868 to 1874. Though not remaining in office long enough to see this particular Act pass through Parliament and gain Royal Assent, it is to him that the thanks of the army are due for the raft of sensible and valuable reforms that were instigated.

26. Blackamoors as Drummers

That negro drummers, were at one time, the pride of many a famous regiment, is not disputed, yet their introduction and history is difficult to trace. Influences from the East have made themselves felt on more than one occasion throughout the history of military music. The Saracen kettle drums, tabor and cymbals or the craze for Turkish bands and instruments being more obvious examples. H.G. Farmer's *The Rise and Development of Military Music* indicates that:

"The great general Frederick the Great (1712-1786) was one of the first to introduce percussion instruments into his regimental bands and so impressed was he with the imposing appearance of the oriental musicians that he engaged turbaned and bedizened negroes to manipulate them."

One of the earliest known instances of the introduction of black drummers into English regiments is contained in *The History of Thomas Farrington's Regiment*, the 29th Foot, later to be the 1st Worcestershire Regiment. They had recruited black drummers in

1759 but under curious and not altogether tasteful circumstances. The following account is taken from their Regimental History:

> Admiral Boscowan being at the surrender of Guadaloupe and thinking that blacks would prove very ornamental as drummers procured eight or ten boys whom he brought home and gave to his brother who then commanded the 29th Regiment. The King's permission was obtained to retain them in that capacity and there are records to show that the custom of having black drummers continued for the better part of eighty-four years, the last one died on 15th July 1843.

It is possible that black drummers in English regiments were around much before the 1759 date since Farmer alludes to having seen a painting of the Battle of Blenheim, August 18th 1704, which depicts a black kettle drummer. A black trumpeter is shown in State Dress of the Royal Horse Guards, circa 1742, in Richard Simkin's *Our Armies*. Not only were black drummers employed by many regiments, they appear, in some, to have been quite numerous; up to sixteen being quoted.

They were used not only as time beaters but also performed on triangle, tambourine, cymbals, kettle and tenor drum and often with an instrument called the 'Jingling Johnnie'. This consisted of a pole or staff surmounted by several crescents (possibly due to Turkish influence?) and hung about with hundreds of small bells. Often they would be bedecked with plumes of feathers and long tails of coloured horse-hair. The drummers who played these instruments were dressed in the most ornate and elaborate uniforms with brightly coloured, slashed tunics and high feathered turbans; expense appeared to be no object. The following, taken also from the history of the 29th and dated 1834, gives an indication of the splendour of their attire:

> Full dress: A muslin turban with a silver crescent in front, surmounted by a scarlet hackle feather twelve inches long, with silver cord and tassel entwined around the turban. A silver plated stock for the neck which opened with a clasp and fastened from behind. Yellow cloth jacket, Hussar fashion, trimmed with black fur on the collar and cuffs, the breast was embroidered with black silk cord, and three rows of silver buttons in front. This jacket was worn open. The waistcoat was of white cloth embroidered with crimson cord, and had a row of silver buttons down the front. With a yellow and crimson silk sash round the waist, they also wore Turkish Scimitars, brass scabbards with sling waist belts. The pantaloons were scarlet with a broad silver stripe on the outside seams, and fitted tight at the knee. Yellow Hessian boots with large black silk tassel in front. The dress on other occasions was a bearskin busby, with a yellow bag, worsted tassels and line, with scarlet feather. Jacket and waistcoat as above. Silver grey coloured trousers with yellow stripes down the outside seams.

In some regiments, white gauntlets were worn, whilst in others, tight fitting white gloves were worn to contrast the black fur cuffs.

The Foot Guards too, followed the trend, and there is anecdotal evidence to be found in the history of the Coldstream Guards regarding a black drummer named 'Billy Blades'. He apparently served with the regiment for many years and retired, in good health in the mid-1800s. The Life Guards too went in search of a black drummer, and identified one particularly handsome fellow, very tall with a fine natural physique. Considerable sums of money were spent by the Life Guards in negotiating his procurement, only to find that their ideal black drummer was totally amusical and was possessed of no sense of rhythm whatever. Shortly after his procurement, he had to be let go.

In time, black drummers began to decline in number and their role as 'musicians' diminished to being little more than that of a regimental mascot. Regiments still competed with one another though, to produce the smartest and most elaborately dressed black drummer to march at the head of their drums and fifes, or in some cases to act as the time beater.

The cost of their clothing was borne by the regiment's officers; always a heavy burden; but with such competitiveness it became a serious financial drain on an officer's purse.

Little now remains to remind us of the antics and the splendour of these black drummers. The wearing of leopard or tiger skins in some regiments by tenor and bass drummers might be connected as might the twirling of the tenor and bass drum sticks; each perhaps a survivor of the time when spectacle and pageantry were of greater value than musical ability.

27. The Drum Major – a Historical Precedent

A Drumme is one the necessariest officers to a Company, and divers passages of weaight and moment hee is to be employed in, for many times they are sent to parlie with the Enemie, and to redeeme Prisoners from the Enemie, therefore hee ought to bee a man of personage, faithful, secret and trusty. He ought to speak several languages, especially the Drumme of a Colonels Company ought to be this qualified, he had the command of all Drummes of the Regiment, and upon a March he appoints every Drumme his place, and time to beate, using a due proportion to every one for their time of relief. In a Campe or Leaguer, no Drumme must offer to beate for the releaving of the Watch before the Drumme Major first begins. Most usually he is sent on all employments too, and from the Enemie, hee ought to have a small Drumme for lightnesse to carry with him, hee is also to Have a paper wherein is write the Contents of his Message, which is to be placed upon his Hatte. When he approache neere the Enemies Towne, hee is to make a stand a Musquet shot from the Ports and to beate a Parley, whereby they may know his intent, hee ought to be of singular good carriage, and discreet to observe and take notice of passages, that may give any intelligence to his officers of the state of the Enemie. Hee must be very wary that nothing be screwd from him, neither by fayre nor foul meanse, wherefore he must be wary of the Enemies friendship, in bestowing courtesies upon him especially in giving him drinks, least in hiss cups he reveal any secrets. When a Drumme is sent out of the Enemies Campe he must not be suffered to approach neere the Guards nor ports until an officer be sent unto him (who must bee attended with a Guard of Musquetires) and having blind folded him he is to be conducted into the Campe of the Generalls Pavillion where a guard must passe on him least he should discover the weaknesse of the Campe. A Drumme ought daily in the day time in time of peace, frequent the Guards and beate to the souldiers, that they may distinguish, and know one kind of beate from the other (Viz) a Call, a March, a Troope, a Charge, an Allarm, a Retreit etc., He ought to passe precisely upon the hours appointed for the releeving of the Watch, to beate their Drummes for the summoning of the souldiers together, and to doe such other duties as shall be required, he must be obedient to his Captaine, and the rest of the Officers whensoever they command him to goe, or stand, or to beate any point of warre, every Company ought to have two Drummes at the least.

Taken from *The Principles of the Art Militarie* by Henry Hexham (1637).

Historically the appointment of Drum Major was not officially recognised and adopted until as late at 1810, though as we have seen from Chapter 7, the possible creation of the office dates back to 1507.

Prior to the creation of the rank of Warrant Officer in 1881, the ranks of Staff Sergeant First Class and Staff Sergeant Second Class existed for the senior personnel within the infantry. Among the holders of the rank of Staff Sergeant First Class were to be found The Regimental Sergeant Major, The Regimental Quartermaster Sergeant (RQMS) and The Orderly Room Quartermaster Sergeant (ORQMS) – all of whom wore distinctive four bar chevrons on the upper arm, point downwards. Staff Sergeants Second Class, which included, Drill Sergeants (Foot Guards battalions) and Company Sergeant Majors in both Foot Guards and Battalions of the Line, appear to have worn the rank badge of a Colour Sergeant. This consisted of three chevrons and a crown, or in the case of the Foot Guards, three chevrons and a colour badge, much as their colour sergeants wear today in full dress uniform.

The Drum Major, though never ranking higher than Staff Sergeant Second Class was, due to his perceived importance as the man invariably leading the battalion on the march, always dressed as a Staff Sergeant First Class, being entitled to wear four bar chevrons on his uniform. The privilege of leading the regiment on the march had long been that of the Drum Major. Curiously, it was not apparently made official until the issue of an order of 1803, which sought to offer advice regarding the conduct of long route marches and the problems that might accrue from such activities. The same order also covered the duties of the band and drums. It appears that by the time of the issue of this order, the band and the Corps of Drums of a regiment had come to be considered as quite separate musical entities, each playing in turn whilst on the march. To this end, the order of 1803 decreed that the band – then still termed 'The Musick' – was to be frequently practiced with the Corps of Drums – usually termed simply 'The Drums' – in order to ensure that when on the march and playing alternately, the correct time or measure might be maintained, one to the other without deviation. Furthermore, the order specified that the Drum Major was to take charge of the practice and not the Musick Master. To a certain extent, this precedent remains extant today, where once on parade, the Drum Major commands and leads the band and drums, regardless of the rank or status of the band master or director of music. Even in the Foot Guards, this remains so; the Director of Music, whether a captain, major or, as is often the case for the senior Director of Music, Guards Division, a lieutenant colonel, all march within the ranks of the band and conform to the drum major's commands and signals – only however, whilst on parade.

Certain appointments were considered to be 'Battalion Staff' appointments, which were distinguished by the entitlement to wear a sword; witness latterly (and particularly in battalions of the Foot Guards), The Master Tailor, The Master Chef, (Pre ACC) The Orderly Room Sergeant/Colour Sergeant (Pre AGC) and of course, The Drum Major.

With the advent of the title of Warrant Officer in 1881, came the familiar rank badges of the Royal Arms (RSM), crown within a laurel wreath (RQMS/ORQMS/TQMS/

QMSI) and the crown of the WOII/CSM. The Drum Major however, retained the honour of wearing the four bar chevrons of the former Staff Sergeant First Class, though now inverted and worn point uppermost on the forearm.

The following should be considered when appointing non-commissioned officers into the place and privilege of Drum Major.

Duties and responsibilities of the Drum Major
(For consideration for incorporation into Regimental or Battalion Standing Orders)
Selection Criteria:
1. The appointment to the office of Drum Major is to be considered as a 'Battalion Staff Appointment'.
2. The Drum Major is to be of the rank of Sergeant, Colour Sergeant or Warrant Officer Class II upon appointment. (Acting ranks may be considered at the discretion of the Commanding Officer.)

Status:
3. Due to historical precedent, the Drum Major is to be afforded equal status to that of other Warrant Officers Class II, with the appropriate responsibilities and privileges.

Responsibilities:
4. The Drum Major is responsible to the Commanding Officer for the following:
   - Operational efficiency of the Corps of Drums.
   - Maintaining the Corps of Drums operational, established vehicles and weapons.
   - Maintenance of the music library, documents, instruments and associated equipment and full dress uniform.
   - For ensuring, in conjunction with his superior or any other officer, the welfare of his drummers.
   - Maintaining the level of musical competence, both individually and collectively of the Corps of Drums.
   - Discipline, drill, esprit de corps and turnout of the Corps of Drums on all occasions.
   - Ensuring that all routine bugle calls are sounded on time and correctly – this to include Drum and Flute duty as appropriate to regimental custom.
   - When on the march with the battalion or other formed bodies of the battalion, that the correct marching pace is maintained.
   - Ensuring that the traditions, customs and history of the Regiment in general and the Corps of Drums in particular, are documented, understood and maintained.
   - Maintaining the register of Colour Belt fittings for the ensigns of the battalion; maintenance and cleaning of colour belts; provision and maintenance of colour cases and the detailing and training of drummers for colour casing/uncasing duties.
   - Maintenance of the Battalion clocks

Hierarchy of Succession:
5. The Drum Major is to ensure that appropriate Non Commissioned Officers of the Corps of Drums are suitably trained and capable of deputising for him

in his absence. Furthermore, he is to ensure that any Non Commissioned Officer recommended for appointment to Drum Major, is trained to a level commensurate with taking up that appointment.

28. The English Duty – Drum and Flute Duty

By 1747 the re-adoption of the fife was universal throughout the regiments of Foot Guards and Infantry of the Line. With the fife's rise to its former zenith came a plethora of fife manuals in print, all purporting to be the 'Compleate' (Complete) system for the instrument. Even a cursory glance at a random selection of such publications reveals a striking similarity of content. The table offered below lists only the standard duty tunes but all fife tutors carried a myriad of popular quicksteps, marches and music for playing during Tattoos and Troops etc. It is clear that plagiarism was alive and well in the world of the eighteenth and nineteenth century compilers and printers.

This random selection of fife and drum tutors ranging from 1756 to 1815 was compiled and printed as follows:

1756	Printed and sold by David Rutherford – London
1759/60	Printed and sold by Thompson and Son – London
1767	Printed and sold by Thos. Bennett – London
1770	Printed and sold by C & S Thompson – St Pauls Churchyard – London
1777/8	Printed and sold by Longman, Lukey and Broderip – London
1780	Printed and sold by J Preston – The Strand – London
1780	Printed and sold by T. Skillern – London
1804	Printed and sold by H Andrews – Lambeth – London
1805	Printed and sold by George Willig (believed to be a reprint of a tutor by Michael Hillegas ca. 1776)
1815	Compiled and sold by Samuel Potter – London

Two further examples of printed tutors not shown in the above list merit coverage namely *The Young Drummer's Assistant* ca. 1760 (for drum only) and the rather grandly titled *Drum and Flute Duty for the Infantry Branch of the Army with Instructions for the Training of Drummers and Flautists* – this latter, by Potter is, validated by the War Office, Horse Guards and dated 1st October 1887 – printed, published and available direct from Her Majesty's Stationary Office (HMSO) and selected bookshops.

The Young Drummer's Assistant is believed to be the first drum tutor to use recognisable musical notation in its tablature, even to the extent of indicating which strokes are to be beaten on the drum using the left hand or right hand. There are three pages of instructions relating to the correct method of holding the drum sticks along with explanation of the notation and how it should be interpreted and beaten, followed by a further ten pages of duty tunes. The note forms are mainly quavers, crotchets and minims with certain hieroglyphics for particular execution, e.g. flams, drags and dynamics. Where rolls occur in the music they are written out in full, hence a five stroke roll will be written showing all five strokes which is confusing for nine or eleven stroke rolls, unlike the modern day notation using cross strokes on note tails. The Potter *Drum and Flute Duty* publication is set out in two main parts. Part 1 Section I – deals with duty calls for drum only. These are for such as battalion parades, spring drills and calls for duty in camp, quarters and in the field. Part

Table of Fife Tutors and Duty Tunes/Calls (1756 – 1815)

Date/tune	1756	1760	1767	1770	1777/8	1780	1799	1804	1805	1815
Reveille	✓	✓	✓	✓	✓	✓	✓	✓	✓	✓
Drummers call	✓	✓	✓	✓	✓	✓	✓	✓	✓	✓
Troope	✓	✓	✓	✓	✓	✓	✓	✓	✓	✓
Risings	✓	✓	✓	✓	✓	✓	✓	✓	✓	✓
Singlings	✓	✓	✓	✓	✓	✓	✓	✓	✓	✓
Doublings	✓	✓	✓	✓	✓	✓	✓	✓	✓	✓
Assembly					✓	✓	✓	✓	✓	
Grenadiers march		✓	✓	✓	✓	✓	✓	✓	✓	✓
To arms	✓	✓	✓	✓	✓	✓	✓	✓	✓	✓
Pioneer march	✓	✓	✓	✓	✓		✓	✓	✓	✓
Foot march	✓	✓	✓	✓	✓	✓	✓	✓	✓	✓
Tattoo	✓	✓	✓	✓	✓	✓	✓	✓	✓	✓
Retreat	✓	✓	✓	✓	✓	✓	✓	✓	✓	✓
The general	✓	✓	✓	✓	✓	✓	✓	✓	✓	✓
Dead march	✓	✓	✓		✓				✓	
Rogues march								✓		✓
Scotch duty	✓	✓	✓	✓	✓	✓	✓	✓		

1 Section II – covers the complete list of Drum and Flute Duty calls from the Drummers' Call to the National Anthem. Part 2 Sections I, II and III offer training for drummers in Music Theory (I), Instructions and Exercises for Drummers (II), and Instructions and Exercises for Flautists (III). Printed using modern notation and running to ninety five pages, it is by far and away the Rolls Royce tutor of its day. But what of the duty tunes listed above? Some explanation might be useful.

Reveille: (AKA The Long Reveille) From the French 'reveil' to wake up, however the French tend to prefer the title 'The Diana' in reference to the Roman soldiers being woken to the sound of the horn of Diana, the goddess of hunting. The Reveille is known and titled throughout all fife and drum tutors as 'The Mother and the three camps' and many have been puzzled as to why it is so named and where (if anywhere) the divisions in the music might occur. The tune is structured as follows:

The first sixteen bars are often quoted as the 'Mother' – this title possibly indicating the 'Alma Mater' status of the regiment? The true origins sadly, are lost to us. What then of the three camps? Again the title is lost in time but may be a reference to the lodging arrangements of regiments in the 17th and 18th century where soldiers occupied lodgings in the towns, in ale houses, inns or private accommodation in 'regimental' streets (camp one?) the sergeants and colour sergeants occupying more up market but separate accommodation (camp two?) and the Commanding Officer, Officers, Ensigns and Colours being lodged in the best accommodation available (camp three?).

Such speculation (and it is no more than that) regarding the origins and division of the music into neatly identifiable sections to represent the separate camps, is further made fraught by differences in the music notation where time signatures might typically be simple duple time i.e two crotchets or two minims to the bar, or simple quadruple time with four crotchets to the bar. The Potter tutor of 1887, as do many tutors previously, gives the full title to the piece at the heading whilst a publication titled the *Bandsman – Course of Instructions for Military Musical Instruments* (Book 17 – The Fife Major) dating from ca. 1856, lists all the duty tunes and affords the first sixteen bars of the reveille as "Tune – The Mother", the remaining bars being designated "Tune – The Three Camps". The mystery remains.

One thing that is certain is that the French composer Delibes, for the entr'acte to act three of his tragedy opera *Lakme* – included the Mother and the Three Camps played on a solo fife.

Drummers' Call: Still universally used by drummers, in particular as a part of the Queen's Birthday Parade where a lone side drummer detaches himself from the massed bands and drums to beat the Drummers' Call at the right of the Escort for the Colour. Over time and without the accompaniment of the fife, the Drummers' Call has come to be beaten 'prestissimo' rather than 'moderato' thus losing some of its gravity and accuracy of the call's notation.

Troope: All soldiers to parade for roll call and inspection. Here tasks such as picquet duties and routine daily taskings along with musketry and pike drills would be handed out. Some fife tutors have several Troopes listed, others list only one. However, it is likely that a Troope could occur up to four times daily if only to maintain control over soldiers who might otherwise abscond to visit the local taverns and brothels rather than pipeclay their cross belts, service their flintlocks or chop firewood.

Risings (AKA Rising or Raising): This beating is essentially a preparatory or warning order that the Troope or Retreat or Tattoo is about to take place and the soldiers should carry out such actions prescribed as appropriate for the specific duty and to parade by rank and file in their regimental groups. It normally consists of four bars in two four time but six eight time is not unknown. The Risings would be the precursor to all major duty parades of the soldiers' day.

Pause Notes (Three Cheers): The Pause Notes, often used as a form of salute to the senior officer reviewing the parade, would follow on from the Risings. One document ca. 1756 suggests that the choice of Pause Notes should concur with the key signature of the music to be used for the marching display, i.e. if the piece is in G Major so too must be the Pause Notes. Similarly, should the piece be in F Major the Pause Notes should again concur and so on.

Singlings and Doublings: The Singlings and Doublings formed an integral part of the Troope, Retreat and Tattoo ceremonies as follows, for example, a Retreat in the 19th Century: after the Pause notes, the Singlings would be played, followed by an appropriate fife and drum tune. This in turn would be followed by the Doublings, then back to the Singlings leading onto another appropriate tune and so on. The term 'an appropriate tune' indicates any tune in triple time as used to this day for retreat marches. It was and still is current practice for Retreat beating and Tattoo to last no longer than thirty minutes.

The usual form for such occasions is to begin the Retreat with the Pause Notes, then to step off in quick time to a retreat march in three four time. Then there should follow a programme of music with a mix of static and marching displays at the conclusion of which Retreat is sounded on the bugle as the Regimental Flag is lowered.

Strictly speaking Beating Retreat should only be performed by the 'Drums since it is an ancient ceremony that pre-dates the creation of Bands.

Assembly (Assembling): As far as can be determined the Assembly is essentially a procedure and drill that is the same as the 'Raising of the Troope' and is thought to be a remnant of the Scotch duty. The 1767 Tutor printed and sold by Thos Bennett, has it listed as 'Troope or Assembling' with a tune set in three four time extending to three phrases of eight bars duration.

Grenadiers' March: A tune which is alive and well today, not only as a part of the Queen's Birthday Parade where it is to be heard as the Colour is marched or trooped through the ranks but also currently played as the Grenadier Guards march back to and through their barrack gates. Also to be known as 'The Guards Return'. Historically the Grenadier Companies had close ties with the Regiment's Colours especially concerning their security and protection.

To Arms: Simply as the name implies – all soldiers dress, take up their weapons and repair to their fire positions or allotted posts. In particular the colours are to be secured and protected. This specific role was assigned to the Grenadier Company.

Pioneer Call/March: This duty tune is given in various fife and drum tutors as a short four bar phrase in six eight time – repeated; as a two bar beating without time signature or as two phrases repeated. It would have been sounded at least twice daily for the distribution of such as water, fire wood and possibly the issue of rations. Other routine taskings would include repairs to camp structures and preparation and maintenance of officers' and soldiers' necessary houses.

Foot March (AKA The March, The English March or The Old English March): This appears variously in some tutors and in other sources in more than one form; e.g. time signatures range from two two time to three four time. There is an air of speculation about its true identity where one historian might hold it to be the English March and another might say it is a march that all companies march to, except the Grenadier Companies, the latter having their own march.

Tattoo: Inevitably when engrossed in campaigns that are lengthy, for instance the protracted operations in the Netherlands of the 17th and early 18th centuries, there will be certain foreign words or phrases that are picked up, adulterated and absorbed into common usage of the occupying forces. The obvious example in this case being the word Tattoo! Long before the advent of purpose built barracks in which to accommodate troops, it became necessary to make arrangements for the billeting of soldiers with the local populace in whatever accommodation was available; these streets becoming known as 'regimental streets' – quite often these billets were spare rooms in such as ale houses and inns – soldiers of the day being what they were and left to their own devices would readily spend the night carousing and drinking thus rendering themselves unfit for duty in the morning. To mitigate this, the inn-keepers were warned by beat of drum to close up their establishment's shutters and turn off the taps and for the soldiers to repair to their lodgings in good order. The phrase from the Dutch language used was 'doe den tap-toe' meaning literally 'turn off the taps'. By common usage and phonetic adulteration, the phrase became shortened to 'tap toe' and eventually as the single word Tattoo.

The Tattoo was beaten at nine o'clock in winter and ten o'clock in the summer and would be conducted similarly to the Ceremony of Retreat with the accompaniment of Pause notes, Singlings and Doublings etc. In modern times, Tattoo usually takes the form of a musical marching display by band(s) and drums preceded by the sounding of First Post. This will be followed by a suitable mixed marching and playing programme in both slow and quick time, culminating in the sounding of Last Post; the senior guest taking the salute as the Corps of Drums (or band) march off.

The sounding of First Post harks back to the time when the Officer of the Day began his rounds, naturally starting at the 'First (sentry) Post' and ending with the 'Last (sentry) Post' – the intervening time being occupied by the drums beating Tattoo around the regimental streets to warn all and sundry to drink up and repair to their billets.

Retreat: One of the best-known military ceremonies, in modern times has its roots deep in the past. Armies of the 1600s and 1700s largely avoided fighting at night. Such activity, apart from being fraught with danger due to not being able to identify the enemy with any certainty so that a 'Blue on Blue' (friendly fire) incident might well occur; it was deemed ungentlemanly to fight at night. Therefore it became customary for opposing armies to disengage from conflict and withdraw (retreat) from the battlefield to harbour positions, post sentries, light fires, set about preparing evening meals and for the officers a glass or two of malmsey or port to enjoy; for the soldiers a visit to the sutler for a jug of ale and perhaps the acquisition of female company of a type not unknown amongst the camp followers. The bugle call is regularly heard as a part of a full arrangement for military band penned by Captain A.C. Green (1888–1974), who was Director of Music of the Royal Naval School of Music Junior Wing. It was first performed in 1932 by the Massed Bands and Bugles of the Mediterranean Fleet, it now forms a regular part of the ceremony of Beating Retreat. Current practice for Retreat beating and Tattoo is for it to last no longer than thirty minutes. In modern times, it has become customary for the Corps of Drums to present the Retreat as a form of military entertainment usually to co-incide with a Dinner night in either the Officers' or Sergeants' mess, the senior guest taking the salute.

The usual form for such occasions is to begin the Retreat with the Pause Notes, then to step off in quick time to a retreat march in three four time. Then there should follow a programme of music with a mix of static and marching displays at the conclusion of which Retreat is sounded on the bugle as the Regimental Flag is lowered.

Strictly speaking Beating Retreat should only be performed by the 'Drums since it is an ancient ceremony that pre-dates the creation of Bands.

The General: This tune was played as a part of the Reveille sequence on certain days to convey to all the troops that this is the day that the regiment is changing to new quarters and therefore all ranks should ensure that they leave nothing behind in the way of equipment or clothing.

Dead March: This speaks for itself since the playing of a dead soldier to his rest was part of the drummers duty. Of the random selection of fife tutors above it may be seen that not all carried the dead march and furthermore not all the tunes were the same either in key or tempo. In the main the music for the Dead March is drawn from the Dead March in Saul, paradoxically set in two four time rather than the original common time and other tunes simply titled Dead March but set in common time.

Rogue's March (or 'Drumming out air'): See Part 5 Chapter 27 for full details.

Scotch (Scots) Duty: Many of the fife and drum tutors have the Scotch Duty, or certain elements thereof; however with the publication of the *Drum Major's Manual* by Samuel

Potter, ca. 1815, all but the Scotch Reveille tune, known colloquially as 'Old Mother Reilly' has been expunged.

An example of the daily routine set by the English duty might have been as follows:

0600	Drummers' Call DD – FM parades under DM
0630	Reveille FM – Mother and The Three Camps followed by 'Old Mother Riley' (plus the General if moving quarters) – Around Regtl Streets and lodgings
0700	Pioneer Call DD – Collect water, firewood and rations Prep bkfst
0800	Sick parade – Sick report to Surgeon
0830	Drummers Call DD – FM parade under DM
0845	Raising for the Troope FM – Soldiers parade for Troope
0900	Troope – Roll call, inspection, Picquet and fatigues told off, – Parade State to Adjt by Officer of the day.
0945	New Picquet Guard march to Gd Rm led by DD & Fifer to a suitable quick-step – sentries relieved – Remainder carry out routine daily tasks as given
1130	Roast Beef – collect rations – Troops prep mid-day meal
1215	Pioneer Call – Water, firewood etc
1300	Drummers' Call – FM Parade under DM
1345	Assembly – Raising for the Troope – Soldiers parade – colour and escort collected from Guard House and halts at the left flank of the parade ground
1400	Comd Offr comes on parade – receives Regimental Salute – Adjt delivers Parade State – Colour party march on parade – received by present arms – FM plays Point of War – Colonel carries out inspection of Troops – Sjt Major conducts massed arms drill to beat of drum – FM play Regtl March – Troops form Divisions and march past Colonel - Companies fall out and resume routine tasking under Company Comds directions
1600	Pioneers Call – Collect Water, fire-wood and rations as appropriate – prepare evening meal
1800	Retreat – Soldiers form up for ceremony and Roll Call –FM Beat Retreat – this marks the end of the working day – Soldiers fall out and seek recreation
2100/2200[1]	Tattoo is beaten around Regtl Streets to warn all sutlers and ale house proprietors along with the 'Ladys Abbess' establishments to close down and send the drunken licentious soldiery back home, doubtless Having consumed at least their 'Act of Parliament!'[2]
Legend:	DD = Duty Drummer (consisting of duty drummer and duty fifer) – FM = Field Music (Corps of Drums) – DM = Drum Major.

---

1 Winter time 2100, Summer time 2200.
2 A military term for 'small beer' (low or no alcohol beer) five pints of which, by act of parliament a landlord was formally obliged to give each soldier gratis

Coda

This study began by posing three questions relating to the validity of the assumed importance and privileged status afforded to such military musicians as trumpeters, drummers and fifers:
1. Is it true?
2. Upon what basis was this alleged importance founded?
3. When did it all begin?

From the foregoing it is clear that as far back as pre-biblical times, trumpeters, inclusive of rams horns et al, and latterly drummers and fifers (flute players) were a part of the elite and not usually drawn from the populace in general. That they formed an important part of the retinue of kings and nobles is without doubt; hence their elevated status and the associated privileges that accrued to them. As to when it all began is almost impossible to say but in antiquity lies the answer. This book has harked back to 4000 BC and beyond, and has offered evidence of the existence of military signallers from at least that time. It would seem that all armies in all parts of the world have utilized military instruments for acts of worship, adulation and of war. The slow declination of the importance of the military musical signaller being paralleled by the rise in technology and modern military requirements and also the changing face of society both within and without the armed forces. The evolution of the art of drumming has been traced throughout; it is therefore the hope of the writer that it has been covered succinctly and without too much in the way of abridgement.

The role of drummers today is almost entirely ceremonial but nonetheless, many ancient traditions remain embodied in the ethos of corps of drums as the 'shop window' of the battalion. Once again the drums provide a battalion's first line music for all those occasions requiring something special. The connection between the drums and the colours remains firmly established to this day in all regiments, tracing its roots back as far as history can take us. The adulation of dignitaries on state occasions by bugle or trumpet fanfare continues, but perhaps thankfully, the drummer goes to war, not dressed in scarlet and beating a parley under the enemy ramparts, but as a fully professional fighting soldier though still as the proud custodian of the Army's senior music.

Tempting the gods to favour one's own warriors in battle by using the self-same musical instruments as previously used for praise and worship as adjuncts of war, seems to be anathema but by such dubious means were the seeds of evolution sown which created a primitive but powerful voodoo controlled by an elite corps, initially of priests and holy men but, eventually by kings and nobles seeking to create fame and imperial fortune by dint of 'Trumpet, Drum and Fife'.

Sources Cited

Galpin Society Paper on The English March by kind permission of Dr Maurice Byrne
The Young Drummers Assistant (ca. 1760)
'Drum and Flute Duty for the Infantry Branch of the Army with Instructions for the Training of Drummers and Flautists' – validated by the War Office, Horse Guards and dated 1st October 1887
Infantry Drill Manual – 1893
Infantry Training (4 Company Organisation) 1914 War Office
Arbeau, Thoinot, *Orchesography* (1588)
Bennett, Thos., *The Compleat Tutor for the Fife* (ca. 1767)
Blades, James, *Percussion Instruments and their History* (London: The Bold Strummer, 2005)
Cockerill, Art, *Sons of the Brave* (London: Martin Secker & Warburg, 1984)
Derbridge, G., 'Dress of the Drummers of the Three Regiments of Footguards – Charles II (1650–1685)' (*JSAHR* Vol XLII No 172 Dec 1964)
Derbridge, G., 'Dress of the Drummers of the Three Regiments of Footguards' (*JSAHR* Vol I No 205 Spring 1973)
Derbridge, G., 'Dress of the Drummers of the Three Regiments of Footguards' (*JSAHR* Vol LII No 209 Spring 1974)
Grose, Francis, *A Classical Dictionary of the Vulgar Tongue* (London: Printed for C. Chappel, 1811)
Mersenne, *Fifth book of wind instruments* (Proposition XIX p.333 – Table 32)
Murray, David, *Music of the Scottish Regiments* (Edinburgh: Mercat Press, 2001)
Tamplini, G., *The Bandsman* – Book 17- The Fife Major (ca. 1856)
Winstock, Lewis, *Songs and Music of the Redcoats* (London: Leo Cooper, 1971)
The Corps of Drums Society Magazine – *Drummers' Call* (Various)
Internet Sources (Various)

Helion Studies in Military History

No 1   *Learning from Foreign Wars. Russian Military Thinking 1859-73* Gudrun Persson (ISBN 978-1-906033-61-3)

No 2   *A Military Government in Exile. The Polish Government-in-Exile 1939-45, a Study of Discontent* Evan McGilvray (ISBN 978-1-906033-58-3)

No 3   *From Landrecies to Cambrai. Case Studies of German Offensive and Defensive Operations on the Western Front 1914-17* Capt G.C. Wynne (ISBN 978-1-906033-76-7)

No 4   *Playing the Game. The British Junior Infantry Officer on the Western Front 1914-18* Christopher Moore-Bick (ISBN 978-1-906033-84-2)

No 5   *The History of the British Army Film & Photographic Unit in the Second World War* Dr Fred McGlade (ISBN 978-1-906033-94-1)

No 6   *Making Waves. Admiral Mountbatten's Radio SEAC 1945-49* Eric Hitchcock (ISBN 978-1-906033-95-8)

No 7   *Abolishing the Taboo. Dwight D. Eisenhower and American Nuclear Doctrine 1945-1961* Brian Madison Jones (ISBN 978-1-907677-31-1)

No 8   *The Turkish Brigade in the Korean War Volume 1. Kunu-Ri Heroes (November-December 1950)* Dr Ali Denizli (ISBN 978-1-907677-32-8)

No 9   *The Diaries of Ronnie Tritton, War Office Publicity Officer 1940-45* Edited by Dr Fred McGlade (ISBN 978-1-907677-44-1)

No 10   *The Thinking Man's Soldier. The Life and Career of General Sir Henry Brackenbury 1837-1914* Christopher Brice (ISBN 978-1-907677-69-4)

No 11   *War Surgery 1914-18* Edited by Thomas Scotland and Steven Heys (ISBN 978-1-907677-70-0)

No 12   *Counterinsurgency in Africa. The Portugese Way of War 1961-74* John P. Cann (ISBN 978-1-907677-73-1)

No 13   *The Armed Forces of Poland in the West 1939-46* Michael Alfred Peszke (ISBN 978-1-908916-54-9)

No 14   *The Role of the Soviet Union in the Second World War* Boris Sokolov (ISBN 978-1-908916-55-6)

No 15   *Generals of the Danish Army in the First and Second Schleswig-Holstein Wars, 1848-50 and 1864* Nick B. Svendsen (ISBN 978-1-908916-46-4)

No 16   *A Considerable Achievement. The Tactical Development of the 56th (London) Division on the Western Front, 1916-1918* Matt Brosnan (ISBN 978-1-908916-47-1)

No 17   *Brown Waters of Africa. Portugese Riverine Warfare 1961-1974* John P. Cann (ISBN 978-1-908916-56-3)

No 18   *Man of Steel and Honour. General Stanislaw Maczek. Soldier of Poland, Commander of the 1st Polish Armoured Division in North-West Europe 1944-45* Evan McGilvray (ISBN 978-1-908916-53-2)

No 19   *The Gaysh. A History of the Aden Protectorate Levies 1927-61 and the Federal Regular Army of South Arabia 1961-67* Frank Edwards (ISBN 978-1-908916-87-7)

No 20 *The Whole Armour of God. Anglican Army Chaplains in the Great War* Linda Parker (ISBN 978-1-908916-96-9)
No 21 *Wars, Pestilence and the Surgeon's Blade. The Evolution of British Military Medicine and Surgery during the Nineteenth Century* Thomas Scotland & Steven Heys (eds.) (ISBN 978-1-909384-09-5)
No 22 *With Trumpet, Drum and Fife. A Short Treatise covering the Rise and Fall of Military Musical Instruments on the Battlefield* Major Mike Hall (ISBN 978-1-909384-17-0)
No 23 *Battlefield Rations. The food given to the British soldier for marching and fighting 1900-2011* Anthony Clayton (ISBN 978-1-909384-18-7)
No 24 *Railroads and Rifles. Soldiers, Technology and the Unification of Germany* (new edition) Dennis E. Showalter (ISBN 978-1-909384-19-4)